Praise for *Woven Together*

"*Woven Together* is a masterful tapestry. It is precisely what educators need: an articulation of how to lead from the inside-out, true to their most authentic selves, so that they may best serve their students in changing the world."

—**Dr. Anindya Kundu**, sociologist, award-winning educator, and author of *The Power of Student Agency*

"Powerful. Courtney Rose breaks down the steps for those who desire to humanize education and truly maximize their educational reach. Her approach to dismantling systems in order to transform them is a must read."

—**LaNesha Tabb and Naomi O'Brien**, authors, public speakers, and educators

"Courtney Rose's book could not come at a better time for teachers. As more and more educators leave the profession while we deal with the fallout from unforeseen and unprecedented social and political conditions, the need for this book is self-evident. Those of us who remain are looking for the sustainable strategies that Courtney discusses. Administrators who are desperately seeking to recruit new teachers and retain the ones they have can look to this book as a guidebook for how to create conditions that are necessary for teachers to thrive in."

—**Larry Ferlazzo**, high school teacher, author, and Education Week teacher advice columnist

"*Woven Together* by Dr. Courtney Rose is a masterful presentation for all educators, students, and education leaders, with very practical and doable examples of showing up and being your authentic self in one of the most important and sacred spaces, the teaching and learning environment. Dr. Courtney Rose, through her own storytelling and demonstration of *Woven Together*, provides for the reader concrete examples and theoretical contextual insight into some of today's most challenging educational and social issues. *Woven Together* has helped … a higher education executive, it will do the same a… ted to an authentic, trust-based teaching a…

—**Dr. Anthony E. Munroe**, …
Community College / City …

WOVEN TOGETHER

WOVEN TOGETHER

How Unpacking Your Teacher Identity Creates a Stronger Learning Community

COURTNEY E. ROSE

JOSSEY-BASS™
A Wiley Brand

Published by John Wiley & Sons, Inc., Hoboken, New Jersey.
Published simultaneously in Canada.

For general information on our other products and services or for technical support, please contact our Customer Care Department within the United States at (800) 762-2974, outside the United States at (317) 572-3993 or fax (317) 572-4002.

Wiley also publishes its books in a variety of electronic formats. Some content that appears in print may not be available in electronic formats. For more information about Wiley products, visit our web site at www.wiley.com.

Library of Congress Cataloging-in-Publication Data is Available:

ISBN 9781394152131(Paperback)
ISBN 9781394152148(ePDF)
ISBN 9781394152155(ePub)

Cover Design: Wiley
Cover Image: © Daisy-Daisy/Getty Images
Author Photo: Courtesy of the Author

SKY10057243_100923

For Mom and Dad, the first two, and still most powerful, educators in my life.

Contents

Acknowledgments

This book would not be possible without the values, skills, lessons, and gifts passed on to me from the generations of educators, both formal and informal, in my family. I often say that teaching, educating, is the family business and the truth is that this work lives and moves through me in ways that make me feel forever woven together with the grandparents and great grandparents on *both* sides of my family whose strength and wisdom gained in their own journeys to and through educational spaces, whose love, care, and passion for developing the next generation, whose no-nonsense and fearless leadership has shaped who I am and how I engage in this work.

Words cannot express the gratitude I have for my first, and most powerful, educators, my parents, but I will do my best.

Mom, thank you for teaching me the power of my voice and giving me this gift of writing. You bought me my first journal, and in that moment, opened me up to the importance of looking within when the world feels lonely, scary, or chaotic and it has been the greatest source of strength in my life. Growing up I'd watch you from the back of rooms filled with people hanging on your every word as you moved powerfully and gracefully, and I used to pray for just one ounce of what at that time I thought just had to be *magic*. As I've gotten older, I realize that what really fuels you is the deep love for yourself, your family, and your community that is woven into every fiber of your being and I thank you for passing that love on to me.

Your guidance throughout this book journey, and my life, has been invaluable, and with you in my corner, I've been able to navigate it all with so much confidence, power, grace, and peace.

Dad, I always thank you for being a pillar of calm and peace, and I will echo that here. I feel so blessed to have a father who sees and nurtures me the way you have.

But I also want to thank you for contributing to the book as not only one of the featured teachers, but also keeping me grounded in remembering my audience and my why. You entered the K–12 classroom just a little while before I did, and just as with Mom I'd sit in the back of your classroom and watch you pull out the absolute best in each of your students. It's actually why I jumped at the opportunity to be a math teacher when it presented itself during my first year in Jacksonville, which ultimately shaped the rest of my journey as an educator. It's been so special to share this part of our lives with each other, and it's added a powerful element to our father/daughter relationship.

Brandon, thank you for all of the support you've given me throughout the years. You helped me think through and process aspects of this book journey that often don't come naturally to me and helped me feel so protected and cared for. Thank you!

Mariel, I've said this before, but you are the friend/sister whom I prayed for, and it comes as no surprise to me that you and I were writing our first books at the same time. You've held space for me in ways that often created pathways for the words to flow, and my heart just overflows with love and gratitude for the person you are and sisterhood you've brought into my life.

To my other sisters Jessica, Jordan, and Amber, some might not understand the cover art, but you all know that it is symbolic of the place where we all met and formed this lifelong friendship, the place where I had the revelation that I wanted to be a teacher, that it was who I'd probably always been. You all have been by my side through so many milestones and loved me through so many versions of myself. Thank you all for never asking me to be anything or anyone other than who I am.

C, I know I don't need to say much, or anything at all, to let you know the love and gratitude I have for you. Your unwavering love, patience, support, and understanding lifted me up so many times during this writing process.

To the rest of my incredible support system, Maxie, Jenn, Ed, Zo, thank you for the words of encouragement, the laughter, the listening ears when I needed it, the brutal honesty when I needed it, and for always loving me for just who I am.

To my incredible featured teachers: Alexia, Jeff, Bobby, Brian, Vennieta, Tanesha, Dee, Deonna, Ryan, Joscelyn, Yari, and Eva, you all inspire me on a daily basis. I can't express enough how deeply grateful and blessed I feel to have had the opportunity to sit in your brilliance and wisdom. The authenticity, honesty, and vulnerability you each approached our conversations with helped me take this book to new heights and deeper explorations of the issues and *myself*. Thank you. Thank you. Thank you.

A huge thank you to my Jossey-Bass team. Your patience, understanding, and flexibility helped me to produce the book I've been carrying in my heart for years, and I thank you for seeing the vision and helping me to bring it to life.

I'd also be remiss not to thank my social media family, which constantly posted things like "Write the book, sis!" and "Where's the book, sis?" and encouraged me to sit down and start writing, even before I knew exactly what I had to say.

Thank you to every educator whom I've had. In each of your unique ways, you encouraged me to tap into different aspects of who I am and who I want to be and find my strength and power, shaping the woman and educator I am. Special gratitude to my sixth grade Reading teacher Ms. Koplo, my AP Psych teacher Mrs. Barnett, my high school Spanish teacher Ms. Chandler, and professors Dr. Stephanie Evans, Dr. Yolanda Sealey-Ruiz, and Dr. Christopher Emdin. Each and every one of you created learning environments that allowed your students to just *be*, to remember who we are and opened opportunities to express the fullness of ourselves freely and without judgment and I can see threads of each one of you woven into my own practice.

Finally, thank you to my students, from my first third-grade babies all the way to my grad students. Each and every one of you has shaped the educator, and person, that I am in such profound ways, and I carry each one of you in my heart.

I love you all and I hope you see the gifts, lessons, and love you have all passed on to me woven throughout the words in this book.

Love,
Courtney/Dr. Rose

About the Author

Dr. Courtney E. Rose is a Florida-based teacher, educator, and educational consultant, and founded Ivy Rose Consulting in 2018. Prior to beginning her doctoral studies, Dr. Rose taught fifth-grade math and science in the Duval County Public School system in Jacksonville, Florida (two years of which were completed during her commitment as a Teach for America corps member). At the time of writing this book, she was a Visiting Professor in the Education Policy Studies Department at Florida International University in Miami, Florida. Dr. Rose's research and work interests include the development and implementation of innovative approaches designed to (re)humanize instructional practices, curricular designs, and learning environments. Her student-driven approach to teacher education and development aims to provide teachers with new tools and understandings on how to incorporate students' authentic voices into curriculum and instruction to better engage students with academic content. Adopting a framework rooted in critical self-reflection and collective dialogue, Dr. Rose views curricular designs and instructional practices as powerful tools through which to construct, legitimate, and impose messages about what is appropriate, intelligent, and valuable, which impact both educators' and students' experiences within schools. Given this, her approach to teacher education/professional development aims to help educators and administrators develop or enhance their practices to create humanizing and collaborative learning environments and co-create more meaningful learning experiences *with* and *for* the increasingly racially, culturally, socially, linguistically diverse students and families of today's schools.

Introduction

Sitting down to write this book was a test that I was not expecting. I found myself trying to write a book that I thought people wanted to read, and I forgot the one piece of advice that I often give when people ask me about the journey of writing, which is to write what you need, or what you felt you needed at a given time in your life's journey. As I sit and reflect on that now, the time I've spent in my teaching journey has me reflecting on when I first entered the classroom as a Lead Teacher. That version of myself was so confident.

Remembering

Reflecting back on that first year as a Lead Teacher, I was so excited. I was finally stepping into the world and the work that I felt was what I was meant to be doing, what I was put on this earth to do. We often use words like *purpose*, *calling*, or *destiny* to describe the intensity of this emotion, and this version of myself, this Courtney Rose of the past, felt like I was stepping into all of those things. I was walking in my purpose, answering my calling, and following my destiny, and I could not have been more excited. It did not happen exactly how I thought it would happen, but I was doing it and I was proud of myself because I was going to do something that meant something to me and to the world.

As I entered that first classroom that year, it took only about a week or so before I realized that perhaps this was not going to be or what I was told that it was going to be, what my university-based teacher education program had prepared me for, and I felt myself begin to question the path that I selected. Based on state testing data, the school was identified as the "lowest-performing school in the district" earning the lowest *F* of any of its schools. Given this, the school, which served students from kindergarten through eighth grade and a predominantly Black student population, was labeled a "turnaround school" and became a target for district and statewide efforts to reform the school and improve test performance. This push toward immediate turnaround became the school's entire identity during the year that I joined as a teacher and governed almost every aspect of our daily experiences within the building.

Although 40 humans sat in chairs in front of me every day, my school and classroom started to feel less and less like spaces where *people* came together and more like a lab where practitioners produced and analyzed data. The students, and teachers, were constantly under surveillance. Students were constantly taking tests and being assessed, and by extension, so were the teachers. We, the educators, were observed endlessly, asked to meet at a moment's notice, and required to submit things so that our expertise and "effectiveness" could be measured and evaluated. On any given day, I could expect at least five people to come in my room unannounced, and in front of my students, make comments about what I was not doing well, what I needed to do better, what I should be doing, and what they, who had never spent more than five minutes with my students, thought would serve them best. On one particularly frustrating day, the school was visited by a team that specialized in assessing student engagement. The three-person team spent the morning moving through the hallways peeking through the windows of each classroom door to gather a 30-second "snapshot" of students' engagement with the learning taking place on the other side. At no point did they open the door, enter the classrooms, or speak to any of the students or teachers. It was quite possibly one of the most dehumanizing experiences of my life as we were literally treated like animals in a zoo being viewed through the glass. They then went to a room and compared notes, ultimately creating an overall assessment of how well teachers were engaging students. During the debrief meeting that day, I remember most of the teachers, myself included, becoming increasingly irate as the visitors presented their report, calling out teachers whose classes they found both deeply engaged or disengaged through their analysis of the snapshots.

No matter how long I reflect back on this, which is just one example out of many more, I will never see how this was supposed to benefit us or our students, whose parents often got on ships and left for months at a time as a part of their assignments at one of the two nearby naval bases. They needed something different, something more, and as a community, a school community, we all needed something different. We all needed something more. The burnout was palpable and you could see it on everyone's faces, and experiences like the engagement snapshot observations. We all knew that if we didn't meet the standard that year, the school would look very different, or be closed altogether. You see, during that first year of teaching, my students' parents and families voted on what they thought should happen to the school as one of the reform options on the table was to consider a complete restructuring of the school. This move would likely result in many of the students, and teachers, being displaced to other schools. Having already gone through the previous restructuring that led to the development of the K–8 school to begin with, many of my students began to vocalize that it really did not matter what they did that year because the school probably was not going to be here the next year and so why try? Do you see the internalization of *we do not matter*? I have never felt that so deeply, that I did not matter, that the work I was doing did not matter, that the people, the human beings sitting in the seats that I faced every day, did not matter to so many people whose job description was to communicate the exact opposite.

I barreled through that first year. I struggled and came in every day feeling like a cog in a broken machine rather than a human in a community, which added immensely, immeasurably, destructively to my own personal and professional identity development and vision for myself as an educator. I was an adult, a young adult, but an adult, nonetheless. I could not imagine and I still cannot imagine, what my students were enduring and feeling and the emotions that were rising in them that were not being checked, were not being addressed, were not being tended to in the time that they were in the school building. I started waking up every morning crying, or with this intense feeling of dread, but I would drag myself out of bed, take a shower, get dressed, put on the best smile that I could and just keep on trying every day. I showed up every day because I was walking in my purpose and answering my calling and following my destiny. But I knew it was not right.

One day I got a call to the principal's office. She notified me that I would not be asked to return, but that she did want me to finish the school year because we only had about a month or so left. So, in the middle of the day when I still had students in my room, she called me to the office and gave me this message. What struck me the most, what still sits with me to this day as I think about that moment, are the words she said to me. She said, and I am paraphrasing a bit, "Do not let this place destroy the gift that you have, the passion that you have for this work. You have something. Do not let this place take it." That has stayed with me ever since, and every time I think about it I wonder whether she thought she was *saving* me, and if so, if that place could destroy whatever she saw and thought was worth saving in me, what was it doing to the children in the building? More importantly, what were we, the adults who had taken on this work of serving and educating our students, doing as a community to try to save *them*?

Humanizing Education

I reflect on that year often, and it brings me to tears quite a bit because I know that there was more that I could have done, maybe more that I should have done. But every single day in that building felt like a fight, a battle to hold onto myself and remember why I was there. Ultimately, being fired likely did save me, or at least jolted me back to life and reignited my passion for this work and my purpose in it. I carry those students and that year in my heart because it was one of the most dehumanizing spaces I have ever inhabited. Remembering what it did to the educators in the building, remembering what it did to the students in the building, brings me to tears to this day. I believe it is why I have always focused on how we can create spaces and practices and policies that build our kids up, that see their humanity, and that breathe life into them, but also that recognizes that in order to do that, we need to see the humanity in ourselves as educators and breathe life into ourselves, our colleagues and by extension, our students and their families/communities.

Unfortunately, much of existing education research and policies are framed within deficit-based narratives. The data asks us to look at what isn't working, who is falling short of academic standards, the tactics and approaches that are not effective, and the shortcomings of students, educators, schools, and communities that are not providing or receiving what they need. These narratives have often placed the issues of schooling and educational attainment/academic achievement in students, educators, and communities rather than the systems and structures in which they are contextualized and housed. As a result, many key stakeholders in education (politicians, parents/caretakers, educators, students, etc.) are positioned in direct opposition to each other, creating strong lines of division and fractured learning communities.

Educator, scholar, and author of *We Want to Do More than Survive*, Bettina L. Love writes of the spirit murdering of predominantly Black and Brown youth, along with those whose identities sit outside of the Eurocentric norms that often lie at the root of dominant educational policies and practices. Defining spirit murder as the *denial of inclusion, protection, safety, nurturance, and acceptance because of fixed yet fluid and moldable structures of racism*, and I add, other forms of oppression, those living on the margins are often humiliated, ridiculed, criminalized, and hyper-surveilled for simply *being*. For example, students living in impoverished communities have a greater chance of attending a school that has metal detectors and have their bags searched on a daily basis. Black boys and girls receive harsher punishments for committing the same level, or even less severe offenses, than their White counterparts as are students with disabilities or individualized education plans (IEPs).

As educators, we occupy an interesting position. When we take on the educator identity, we step into a role that places us with one foot on both sides of the coin. We walk through the same metal detectors as our students, but are also tasked with enforcing, often arbitrary, school discipline policies; we experience similar levels of stress and pressure to raise test scores and prove our value within the school building based on how well our students perform, which can lead us to lean into instructional, testing, and grading policies that fuel the false narratives of the tests value, even amid data that prove otherwise. In essence, I argue that the spirit murdering and dehumanizing nature of dominant schooling structures not only dehumanizes students, but educators as well. Speaking personally, in my first year of teaching I felt similar feelings arise in me as I felt when I occupied seats in classrooms throughout my own K–12 schooling. However, this time, I was standing in a position where I had *more* agency, power, and tools to begin to transform that experience, even if only for the time that my students were in my room.

Weaving It All Together

At its roots, I hope this book serves as a tool in the journey toward rehumanizing education and recognizing that, as teachers who were once children/students, as teachers who may also be parents/caregivers, as parents/caregivers of children who are also students, our experiences, both inside and outside of schools, both past and present, are inextricably linked in that they weave together who we are individually and collectively, but they also weave us together to each other in this human experience, and in the experience of teaching and learning. Each of the present-day realities that I cover in this book are informed and shaped by past realities, and have the ability to transform and reshape future realities. Humanizing education starts with recognizing that when I dehumanize you, when I dehumanize a student, or when I sit silently and watch as you are dehumanized, I dehumanize myself. Conversely, when I humanize myself, or act in ways that honor my humanity, I in turn humanize you.

Humanizing education requires the acknowledgment of the daily injustices and inequities that students and teachers, particularly those from and working with communities of color and other marginalized groups, often face. Certainly, any effort to create more equitable and just learning environments for students of color requires that the social, structural, and systemic barriers they face, both inside and outside of their learning environments, be faced head-on. Those bearing witness to discriminatory, oppressive, and exclusionary policies and practices, especially those occupying positions of power within educational and institutional structures, must see it as a professional and personal responsibility to call out these policies and practices while calling themselves and others in to do the work of disrupting, dismantling, and transforming them. This book takes the reader on a journey of weaving all that is necessary together, toward an optimal educational experience for students, parents, and teachers.

Overview of the Chapters

Chapter 1 is where the journey into self begins, posing the question of where teachers' identities overlap with and inform the development of their teacher identity through the construction of the Critical Educational Autobiography. Readers are encouraged to revisit their autobiographies through each chapter, reflecting on what new or deeper insights they have gained.

Chapter 2 presents the ways that language is used to reproduce and reinforce deficit-based narratives and frameworks within dominant educational policies and practices. This chapter encourages a deep-dive into your "why" as educators situate themselves within these narratives.

Chapter 3 also digs below the surface by tackling the numbers and beyond pertaining to recruiting, retaining, and sustaining educators, including a comprehensive discussion of the "invisible tax" that is pushing many teachers out of the classroom.

Chapter 4 explores the notion of intergenerational wisdom and the lessons that should be learned from "those who stay." Contemporary popular depictions of this type of veteran teacher is explored through a frank analysis of the popular television show *Abbott Elementary*, which debuted in 2021, that highlights veteran teacher, Barbara, and all that she brings to the classroom. Further exploration of veteran teachers is also through excerpts of discussions with Featured Teachers.

Chapter 5 takes a different approach in that there is a critical analysis of how the physical body is perceived within educational spaces and how that might impact the ways teachers embody their practice and are unfortunately disembodied.

Chapter 6 focuses on the power of voice and the need to create space for authentic self-expression in the development of self-actualizing learning experiences and environments, and explores the complexities involved in teaching vulnerability.

Chapter 7 widens the scope to weave together teacher and student identities and voices in the development of a student-driven classroom community.

Chapter 8 extends beyond the classroom, inviting teachers to weave together stronger relationships with parents/families/caretakers.

Chapter 9, the final chapter, endeavors to weave together all of the elements of the preceding with a forward-looking approach for the next generation of teachers to come.

Features of the Text

Beginning with Chapter 2, the following elements are included:

Instagram quote: As Instagram is a popular medium of exchanging ideas, especially for educators, and where I have a very substantial following, I start each chapter with a quote pulled from my feed that is primarily devoted to education and teachers.

Featured Teachers excerpts: Additionally, each chapter contains excerpts from my interviews with Featured Teachers. Featured Teachers, in this book, are educators currently or recently serving in K–12 schools, including public, private, and charter.

Reflection questions/activities: The chapters also include reflection questions and activities that are woven throughout the text to encourage ongoing critical self-reflection and revisions to the critical autobiography as previously mentioned.

Appendices: Additionally, appendices included at the end of the book supplement the information shared throughout. These tools include a full description of the critical autobiography assignment, an exercise entitled "Name Story," which serves as both an additional opportunity for critical self-reflection in the development of one's teacher identity and a relationship-building activity that can be completed with students. Additional appendices focus on educational policy analysis, and important acronym, as they relate to the field of education as well as a list of governing bodies to help educators continue to engage in the self-reflective process as they weave together more collaborative instructional practices.

Reference

Love, B. L. (2019). *We want to do more than survive: Abolitionist teaching and the pursuit of educational freedom*. Beacon press.

Chapter 1

Weaving Together Your Teacher Identity

The parts of yourself that you try to leave out of your practice by ignoring or overlooking them are often the parts that impact and shape your practice the most.

Instagram Post
@drcourtneyrose (October 7, 2019)

For many, and I would argue all, educators, the journey to teaching and development of what becomes our "teacher identity" starts well before we declare education as our major or step foot in our first classroom. As educators our reasons for entering teaching and the types of teachers we become can often be traced back to key experiences (both inside and outside of schools/classrooms), people and places spanning our entire lives, the histories of our families and the ties (whether they are weak or strong) to the cultures and communities we identify with and inhabit, and therefore, are intricately woven into the fabric of who we are. Consequently, it should come as no surprise that the development of one's "teacher identity," or how educators come to see and carry themselves as "one who teaches" remains a core area of research, particularly among those aiming to inform, reform, and transform approaches to teacher education.

To dig into the complexities of teacher identity development, this chapter explores two different core components found across existing literature:

- Teacher Identity versus Teachers' Identities
- Identity as Narrative

Additionally, to provide an opportunity for you to weave together your teacher identity development narrative/journey, I break down a commonly used activity, the Critical Educational Autobiography, and some different variations and approaches, many of which I use in my own courses. There are additional journal prompts to help you engage in critical reflection and dialogue if you want to do this activity with members of a Professional Learning Community, grade/content-area team, students, or for your own personal use in your Reflective Teaching Journal.

Teacher Identities versus Teachers' Identities

Existing research shows that the teacher is an integral part of a child's educational experience and is often a primary determining factor in a child's academic trajectory and ultimate professional and social outcomes. However, among this literature there is little agreement on how to conceptualize and operationalize "teacher identity." Specifically, debates arise over where the "self" before and outside their role as an educator intersects and should be considered, if at all. In other words, in the wide range of research on the development and enactment of teacher identities, some key questions remain:

- Where do the teachers' identities, and most importantly their self-image, fit into the teacher identity development process?
- How does who we are, who we're from, and who we want to become impact our perception and development of a "teacher identity"?

Through both my public scholarship via my social media platform and in my courses with pre- and in-service teachers, I find this same tension forcing people into two camps: those who believe that "*teaching is what I do*," and therefore feel a need to separate their personal and professional identities, versus those who believe that "*teaching/teacher is who I am*," and find the two identities to be inextricably linked. I've posed this question in numerous ways, with many teachers reporting a sense that thinking of the role of teacher as "who one is" dehumanizes them and ignores that they are *more* than what they do for a living. For some, this is what leads to the expectation that teachers should *always* be available and makes it challenging for educators to "unplug" and set boundaries without feeling like they're falling short of the professional expectations of their job. On the other hand, some educators feel that viewing teaching as *just* "what one does" *also* dehumanizes educators because it erases their humanity from the process, practice, and art of teaching. Those who hold this perspective find that framing teaching as what one does reduces it down to rote skills and practices that just *anybody* can do, and the justification for scripted lessons and canned teaching approaches that overlook the importance of teacher autonomy, creativity, and relationship-building.

PAUSE, REFLECT, DISCUSS: Framing Teaching and Identity

1. Take a moment to reflect on whether you view your role and identity as a teacher as "what you do" or "who you are."
2. Do you find one more humanizing than the other? Explain.
3. How have these beliefs and framing of your own teacher identity shaped and influenced the way you enact your practice?

Furthermore, scholarship at the intersection of teacher education and teacher identity development notes the number of additional external (i.e., key life experiences) and internal (i.e., emotions) factors that make drawing a clear distinction between a teacher's personal and professional identity nearly impossible. Who we are, or at least how we understand and express who we are, what we think and feel about ourselves and others, what we believe about education and its role in one's life outcomes, is in constant development and evolution as each interaction and experience deepens our understanding of ourselves, the social/political contexts in which we live and learn, and our position within them. Specifically, as we shift from being students to being educators, and gain deeper insight into the political landscape in which teachers must operate, our perception of the field and the work changes. But *how* that changes is not the same from one person to the next.

For the purposes of this chapter, and this book, I ascribe to an understanding of identity, and teacher identity development specifically, as a dynamic process with many mediating factors that render the personal and professional inextricably linked. Olsen's (2008) diagram of "Teacher Identity as Dynamic, Holistic Interaction among Multiple Parts" provides one representation of the multiple points of entry to exploring the formation of one's teacher identity and the ways in which each factor both mediates and is mediated by the others (see Figure 1.1).

However, while this model includes "personal experience," notably missing is "personal identity," which existing research on teacher identity development specifically includes as one's race, gender, social class, sexual orientation, (dis)ability, among other identity markers that likely rise to the surface when one is asked to describe "*who they are*" or "*how they identify*." Nearly *all* dialogue about the so-called "achievement gap," student performance and teacher effectiveness, relies on comparisons across and between these groups (i.e., gap in performance of Black students as compared to

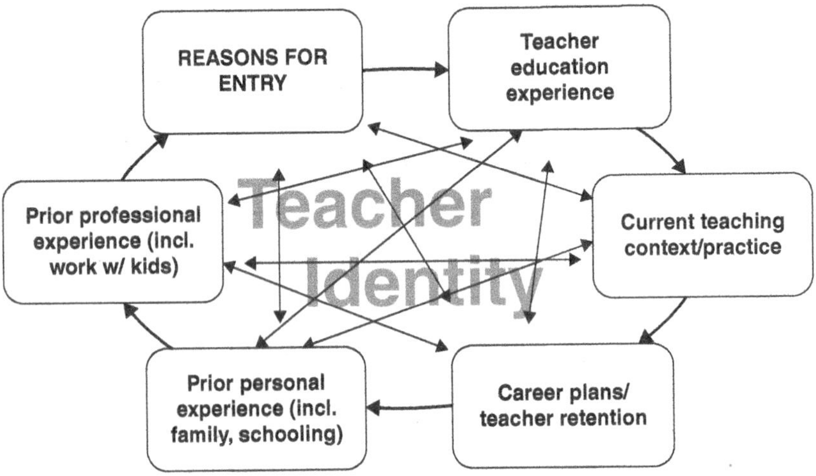

Figure 1.1 Teacher Identity as Dynamic, Holistic Interaction among Multiple Parts.

Source: Reprinted from "How Reasons for Entry into the Profession Illuminate Teacher Identity Development" by B. Olsen, 2008, *Teacher Education Quarterly, 35(3)*, 23. © 2008 California Council on Teacher Education.

their White counterparts or students in low-income schools as compared to students in affluent schools; effectiveness of Black teachers versus White teachers with *x* population). It's only logical, then, that these identities not only impact individuals' perceptions of their identities as students, but also deeply informs and impacts their reasons for entry into the profession and development of a teacher identity. In that regard, not only should "personal identity" be included as one of the mitigating factors in the development of teacher identity, but is actually the filter or lens through which individuals make sense of the other factors. For example, as one's understanding of and relationship to their racial identity and its intersections with their gender and social class identities deepens or changes, their interpretations of their own educational experiences, other professional experiences, prior personal experiences in their families/social groups, and even their career plans might change *drastically*.

Demographic Imperative

It is impossible to discuss the development of one's teacher identity without discussing the impact and influence that identity markers like race, sex, gender, and social class (among others) have on how educators see and are seen within the profession. Doing so ignores how these identity markers were actually used to determine their eligibility for the job in the first place, creating dominant expectations and narratives of the "good teacher." Initially, educators were primarily young, well-educated, white men, most of whom either tutored for individual families or worked part-time, viewing teaching as a pit stop on their journey to higher-paying full-time work in other fields. However, in the late 1800s, access to education expanded in the development of a more formalized and regulated system through common school movement, which would later become the public school system of today. Women were welcomed into the profession as they were believed to have inherently pure and nurturing temperaments, and thus, were viewed as assets as more men looked to find higher-paying and more prestigious jobs, including the newly created educational roles of principals and superintendents. More importantly, it was more acceptable to pay them less—a selling point for the common school movement itself as attempting to staff all of the new classrooms was becoming a costly and challenging endeavor.

The availability of new work options for men and pay differential are widely noted as some of the key factors in the shifting perspectives on the value of teaching, ultimately, a shift toward what is often referred to as the "feminization of education" and the development of the dominant narrative that teaching is "women's work." Consequently, there has been a predominance of female-identifying educators in the K–12 classroom that continues today. The impacts of this shift and narrative can still be seen today as the current teacher population is 76% female, with the largest disparity in the elementary grades where only 11% of the teacher population identifies as male. Conversely, less than 60% of public school principals and about 20% of superintendents were identified as female. While the roots of this particular disparity remains up for debate, it is argued that the perception of women as less capable of providing a certain level of discipline is actually what led to the splitting of classes by age and the placement of men at the helm of older classes or in school leadership positions to handle disciplinary issues. We will return to this in Chapter 3 as we weave together some of the issues that have fueled issues of recruiting and retaining male educators as well as the expectations placed on teachers that fueled one of the largest teacher shortages to date.

Similarly, in the first two decades following the passing of the *Brown v. Board of Education* decision and the racial integration of the nation's public schools, over 31,000 Southern Black educators and thousands of Black school principals lost their jobs leading to a public school teacher population that has remained between 79% and 87% White since the 1987–1988 school year (and one could imagine much earlier than that) with research showing that across the United States, teachers are more likely to be White than their students (Schaeffer, 2021; Ingersoll et al., 2021). In reviewing these demographics and their persistence over *decades*, it is clear that much of our perceptions of what, and who, a teacher is/should be is rooted in the perspectives and models of an overwhelmingly White and female reference point. Therefore, it's easy to see how anyone who identifies differently or has seen and been seen differently in the world (especially in their own student experiences throughout K–12) might bring conceptualizations of the self and the teacher role/identity that are vastly different from the dominant conceptualizations and models, making it challenging to identify *with* the dominant perceptions of the position itself.

This also comes into play if we interrogate how we use the words *personal* and *professional* to describe the various components of our identities as they relate to our work as educators. For example, much of existing research on teacher identity explicitly states a focus on discussing the development of a teacher's "professional" identity. Again, looking at the historical demographic data just presented, it begs the question of what is considered "professional" and who makes this decision. If teacher professionalism is based on the dominant and historical representations of *who teachers are*, then once again, dominant conceptualizations of "teacher professionalism" are rooted in a predominantly White and female *enactment* of the role that may cause a rift between how one sees themself enacting the role of teacher and how they are expected to enact the role.

Disrupting from Within

There are countless stories of educators receiving pushback, being reprimanded or even fired, or deciding to leave because of the constant ridicule and punishment they receive for attempting to bridge the cultural gaps between the culture of schooling and their students. These teachers who go against the grain through their enactment of their practice understand, and often personally experienced, school as places where those who were deemed culturally different (or deficient as we will cover in Chapter 2) were not able to *be who they were* within the cultural/social norms and practices of schooling. For some, this motivates their decision to go into the teaching profession, producing a teacher identity as a *disrupter* aimed at shifting and transforming these dominant beliefs, practices, and norms to create a *different* experience for current/future students. This reality is most often noted among educators of color.

The lack of educators of color, particularly Black educators, and/ or those with adequate experience living and being in racially, ethnically, socioeconomically and linguistically diverse communities, combined with a politically charged education landscape, often results in contentious environments for educators attempting to enact antiracist and culturally relevant practices, particularly for those who sit at the intersections of multiple historically disenfranchised identities (Allison, 2008; Ladson-Billings, 2005). Factors such as perceived biases during recruitment and hiring processes; accent discrimination; undervaluation of their expertise garnered from both personal and academic experiences; and a plethora of other social and political issues at the school, district, state, and national levels often result in contentious, and toxic, work environments for many educators of color. Teachers of color spend much of their time negotiating and navigating issues of racism and oppression, dealing with microaggressions (and some that are *not* so micro at all) from both fellow educators, administrators, parents, and students questioning their academic intelligence, credibility, and effectiveness as educators, which we will explore in greater depth in Chapter 3.

Consistently working under these conditions leaves many educators of color, and others living and teaching at the intersections of social inequities and injustices, feeling isolated and unsupported, making it difficult for them to feel free to enact their authentic identities within an environment that already views them as "too much," "less than," or "insufficient" in many ways. Given these pervasive and persistent structural and social barriers, those choosing to enact teacher identities that disrupt and challenge dominant approaches utilized within the field exemplifies what feminist and womanist scholars refer to as an *ethic of risk*. Driven by a need for action, educators operating from an ethic of risk possess a moral fortitude and vision that enables them to persevere in what can sometimes feel like a futile pursuit of social justice (Beauboeuf-Lafontant, 2002; Welch, 1990).

Collective and Hybridized Identities and "The Calling to Teach"

Examining the character development in books written by Black women authors such as Toni Morrison and Mildred Taylor, White feminist theologian Sharon Welch (1990) argued that these authors convey an "ethic of risk" in their portrayal of the struggle for social justice and equality as an intergenerational struggle. Inherent within the descriptions of the struggles of these authors' characters (i.e., Morrison's Pecola Breedlove in *The Bluest Eye* and the various community members in Taylor's children's books) is the maturity to understand that "ideals are far from realization and not easily won, that partial change occurs only through hard work and persistent struggles of generations" (Welch, 1990, p. 58). Flipping the lens to education and the development of one's teacher identity, in her exploration of the pedagogy of Black womanist teachers, Black feminist scholar Tamara Beauboeuf-Lafontant (2002) noted a similar sense of moral fortitude and interdependence among educators operating through this same "ethic of risk." According to Beauboeuf-Lafontant, these ancestral ties promoted the development and embodiment of a teacher identity that "rests on a concept of self that is part of rather than apart from other people" (p. 81).

Therefore, educators who enact effective and comprehensive antiracist and culturally relevant education embody an identity informed by an ethic of risk and "see their action as a humble, yet essential contribution to an extensive, collaborative, and enduring project of social change" (Beauboeuf-Lafontant, 2002, p. 83). As a result, they often structure pedagogical practices and classroom environments that directly respond to the needs of their students. Specifically, when operating with an ethic of risk, educators often frame their work as a mission and those who take on this work as having the spiritual resources, and, I add, cultural understandings, to undertake said mission (Beauboeuf-Lafontant, 2002).

Identity as Narrative

My mother keeps large baskets filled with photo albums documenting our lives pretty much since I was born, and even before then because there are albums of both her and my dad's childhoods and their life together before my brother and I came along. Throughout my life I've loved sitting for *hours* and flipping through these albums. I've probably looked through each one a hundred times. One day while curled up in my parents' super comfy black leather recliner, I was flipping through photo albums and came across two photos that made me stop and reflect. One was of me at about two or three years old in colorful overalls, hair in pigtails with red bows and barrettes, and holding a bottle with a *huge* smile on my face. The second was taken probably about five years later. I'm on a beach and my hair is pulled into a side ponytail with the hair out in beautiful natural curls. I'm wearing a two-piece bathing suit and posing with my hand on my hip and leaning over to the side. I bet it was a pose we'd done in one of my dance classes. Again, I've seen these photos hundreds of times, but on this particular day I couldn't stop staring at them. There was just something so striking about the carefree joy and light that came through in my eyes and body language. I love looking at pictures of little me, before the self-doubt and insecurities set in, before society taught me that my hair and my body weren't good enough, before my love for learning was challenged by school—where my parents put more than one teacher in line for trying to dim my light by questioning my intelligence. I love looking at pictures of little me because it's just. . .ME! In many ways I feel like my whole life has been, and still is, a journey back to her. I am so grateful to my parents for taking the time to carefully capture and catalog so many moments in my life, and in our collective life as a family. I've reflected many times on why it is that I love sitting and flipping through those albums so much (I've since created many physical and digital albums of my own), and it's only recently that I realized this is one of the ways that I have started to put together my story, to figure out who I was, better understand who I am and use that to inspire and inform the constantly changing vision of who I want to become, both inside and outside of my professional roles.

Consequently, it's in looking back that I begin to unearth experiences and interactions that have shaped and informed my teacher identity, my philosophy of teaching and learning, and my instructional/pedagogical approaches in really profound ways. It is not just a part of my personal identity story but formed *from* it, leaning into Sfard and Prusak's (2005) conceptualization of identity as narrative. Specifically, I find that it is in how educators tell their narratives of their teacher identity development that sheds light on how they identify with and within the field and provides the key to understanding the why behind how they enact their practice.

In a field that relies so much on the *external* evaluation and assessment of their effectiveness *as* an educator, encouraging self-evaluation, self-assessment, and self-reflection through self-narrative can liberate them from reductive views of traditional models of "teacher" and revealing patterns of their personal power, passions, and unique talents that can help them to construct more authentic, holistic, and *humanized* teacher identities. As an example of the powerful threads of humanity that come through in these teacher identity narratives, check out featured teachers Bobby, Ryan, and Eva's sharing of how they set out on the journey of becoming teachers.

FEATURED TEACHERS: Journey to Teaching

Bobby

Teaching happened kind of by circumstance and passion. I went to a college in North Jersey, and when I went there, it was primarily because they recruited me to play basketball. So, there were two options for me that I was interested in. First was architecture, architecture and industrial design. I wanted to put together the fact that I could draw pretty well and math pretty much came easy to me. So, I wanted to put those two things together. The other side was teaching because up until college, I always worked summer camps, and was just great with kids and things like that. So, I enjoyed that. And so when I got to college, I first went to the industrial design program, because your first semester is just like, everybody takes the same classes anyway. So, I had some time. When I went to go to declare a major, I found out that all the industrial design classes took place in the evening, because they had people who were working in the field actually come in, so it was all night classes. And I'm like, do I want to give up basketball? I don't want to give up basketball. So, that's the circumstance part. But the passion part was, I enjoy young people. I enjoy those "aha" moments, building relationships. You know, there are students who I had in summer camp who still reach out to me to this day. Those types of things keep me going and kind of got me into

(continued)

(continued)

the profession. I was not willing [at that time] to give up basketball, and I could get the best of both. It wasn't like teaching was a second choice. It wasn't like it was what was left over for me. I was like, either one of these things can work. It was a win-win for me. So that's what I did.

Ryan

It's very vivid, in my mind, the point where I made a decision that I was going to be a teacher, and that happened in high school. I was in an English class or honors English class, Mrs. J was a teacher. At the front of the room, there was a sign that said "silence is golden," and that was the room, that's the room that we functioned in and it was straight rows and quiet. . .and not human. It was a worksheet-driven lecture, if you make a peep, detention, and I got combative in my own mind. I was like, "Yo, I could do what she's doing better than she's doing it." It's strange because that happened to me very, very young. But still, in that moment, like I was gonna be a basketball player, I was gonna be a rapper. That wasn't the moment where it was solidified that I was going to become a teacher. But that's where the seed was planted, and a lot of my work right now revolves around justice and educational spaces. I didn't have the language to name it, then. But I could feel it. I could feel it specifically in this classroom with this White woman educator where silence is golden, and I had so much noise in me that I wanted to get out. So, I remember just thinking like, kind of on that competitive tip, just thinking to myself, I could run this class better than her. If I ever decide to become a teacher, it's not gonna feel anything like this. I carried that with me. So, then I moved into working on my undergrad work, which is a degree in English. But I had to make money to pay for my books and stuff, and so I applied for this job at the Writing Center, as a writing tutor, and a tutor of Asian philosophy. That's where I was getting my first taste of teaching because here I am this young, 18-year-old, and I got like people that are in their 20s/30s coming through and I'm tutoring them, and they come back. They're actually having great experiences, and I was doing it not the way that Mrs. J did it. You know what I mean? The connections that I made were very human. Like, y'all let me be a partner with you in this journey and let me learn from you in the process, too. So that's how I was vibing with folks. Then, I saw the evals. The highest credential you can get is the stories your students and their families tell about you. Forget about all the other credentials. That's it in my world, and they were telling some good stories about me. I was like Oh, snap, maybe I could do this. Maybe I could teach English. At the same time, hip-hop was happening. It was like Blackstar, it was Tribe Called Quest, the love movement, people hated it, but it was dope. I was becoming more and more fed by educators that didn't exist within the confines or within the ideals of what a teacher is supposed to look, sound, and feel like. I was being educated by the Lauryn Hills of the world, the Mos Def and Talib Kwelis of the world. So, that was vibing with some of that animosity I still had based on my own experience of what I never wanted to be like as an educator with a new discovery as to like, Yo, I can actually be effective and I don't have to do it in the way it's always been done.

Eva

The first example that I had of a teacher that made me think about teaching as something that could be enjoyable was in third grade. I don't remember her name, but her face is clear as day in my head right now, and she just cared so deeply. I was going through so much stuff in my personal life, not living with my mom, living with my grandmother, visiting my dad on the weekends, all of these things that were happening. She came to my church recitals, and she just made such a concerted effort to make me feel seen. I remember playing teacher a lot after that, wanting to have my sibling sit down, and pretend I'm the teacher and I'm in charge and those sorts of things. Then, I went to high school and was like, I don't know how y'all do this job. It looks

(continued)

(continued)

horrible. You don't get paid enough, being a teacher is stupid. I was very anti-becoming a teacher, and it wasn't until my junior year of college where I had an internship, and at that point, I thought I was going to be a mental health counselor so I was working at an alternative sentencing program that had educational services, but they also had mental health services, social workers, things like that. I planned on working on that side of things, until they were like, we don't have a teacher right now. We need you to kind of help out with our HSC students. And I was like, Well, I mean, I'm here, you're paying me, I gotta do what you tell me to do. After three weeks, I was like, this is what I'm supposed to be doing. It was just such an enjoyable experience. I had students that were younger than me, students that were older than me, students that weren't coming in consistently, students that were coming in with a baby, there were just so many different things. To see them so hungry to pass this exam and to have this paper that would open up opportunities for them was just. . .it was great. It was also great to see them come in just really wanting to understand the process and wanting to be able to engage with the actual learning. From there, I applied to Teach For America because I wanted to be in the classroom as soon as possible. I knew I had my own personal issues with the organization and different things that they do, and I said those things in my interview. I was very clear that TFA was just the way to get me into the classroom as quickly as possible, because I knew that I wanted to be engaging with people. I knew that I had the experience to do it. I knew that I had so much to learn, but I was ready to be in the classroom. That was my journey, my trajectory into becoming an educator. Around that same time, I started Black on Black Education, so I was still in undergrad. But I knew that I wanted to understand what it was like to be an educator, what it was like to be a Black educator serving Black students and Brown students. I was consuming information, reading all the books, reading the articles, talking to people who've done this much longer than I have, and during the thick of the pandemic, September 2020, I became a teacher.

Reflect and Discuss

1. In what ways did taking on the role and identity of *teacher* serve as a means to weave together the various pieces of who Bobby, Ryan, and Eva are? Where do their conceptualizations of the teacher identity intersect with their personal identities, passions, and interests?
2. Briefly map out your own journey to teaching. Highlight the aspects of *who you are* that come through in this journey and their intersections with *who you are (or hope to be) as a teacher*.
3. Reflecting on these narratives and your own journey into teaching, are your perspectives on framing teaching as who one is versus teaching as what one does changed? Explain.

Constructing *Your* Teacher Identity Narrative: Critical Autobiography

Each semester, I start my courses with an exploration of identity and self that we weave throughout the semester. This work starts with the completion of the critical autobiography, which takes students on a journey of weaving together the core components of their identity, ultimately ending in their philosophy of teaching and vision for themselves as educators. The assignment is broken down into the following five sections:

- Cultural/Social Identity and Family History
- Key Educational Experiences
- Socio-political Context
- Journey into Teaching
- Philosophy of Teaching/Vision for Yourself as an Educator

Weaving together the key components of their selves and stories, on the background of the sociopolitical context in which they experienced their cultural, social, and academic development, encourages students to identify the underlying beliefs and narratives about themselves, others, education, and society that have informed their journey into teaching and their vision for their role within it.

While it is difficult to find the specific origins of the critical autobiography, the form that I am referencing here has history in sociology, particularly in studying/teaching the Sociology of Education. The critical autobiography looks to the power of storytelling, asking the author to recount key experiences and interactions that have shaped who they are while applying various lenses to excavate the messages they've internalized about race, gender, culture, class, sexuality, ability, and so on. The critical autobiography is an exploration of self that reveals the ways in which our various identity markers have shaped and been shaped by the various experiences and interactions that rise to the top of our minds when we look back on the pivotal moments of our lives. Most importantly, writing and analyzing the critical autobiography forces us to come face-to-face with the ways in which we may have been a part of our own oppression and/or the oppression of others and the damaging narratives, assumptions and biases we may be carrying into our daily interactions, and if left unchecked, our future work.

In her work on the Archeology of the Self, Yolanda Sealey-Ruiz describes this process of facing one's internalized narratives as a process of "excavation," noting that many of these narratives and beliefs are buried deeply within our psyches. Similarly, I view it as a process of unraveling threads that, in many cases, are very intricately woven into the fabric of who we are—so much so that it is hard to identify it as anything other than "just the way things are" or more specifically just who one is.

The excavation or unraveling process is often painful as we must face the ways we were and continue to be complicit in our own and others' oppression, exclusion, and so on. And the perpetuation/evolution of these often damaging narratives, beliefs, and subsequent practices. However, it is in the process of coming to terms with this reality and the vulnerability of sharing this with those we work for and with, that we also come face-to-face with our own humanity. If we have to acknowledge our personal biases and assumptions, our internalized and embodied negative beliefs and practices, then we to have admit that we also have room to grow, things to learn, and we begin to see ourselves as learners just like our students. It requires that we, as educators, engage in a process of moving in and out of the roles of educator and learner, disrupting existing power dynamics and hierarchies that cause rigid expectations of the "student," "educator," and "parent" roles that dehumanize everyone in the process.

Ultimately, there is no single way to approach the critical autobiography. Since the aim is for the authors to dig deeply into their identities, there should definitely be some freedom of choice in how they choose to construct and present it; after all this will give major insight into who they are and how they interpret their past experiences. Some common formats include:

- Traditional narrative essays;
- Journal entries; video diary;
- PowerPoint or Prezi;
- Collages, paintings, or other visual representations of the key themes and ideas unearthed in the exploration of self; and
- Songs, poetry, dance, or other physical interpretations of the key themes and ideas.

No matter how participants/students decide to present their autobiographies, they should be encouraged to focus on two to three key themes that enable them to deeply explore the underlying messages of power and privilege that have informed and shaped their perceptions of self and others. I also recommend asking students to explicitly reflect on and share *why* they chose the specific format they did again since the primary aim is to increase self-awareness and shift into understanding the *why* or *purpose* behind our choices. In some cases, instructors/facilitators will narrow the scope of the assignment down to really drill into a particular aspect of identity development. For example, since I teach courses specifically aimed at exploring education and preparing to step into the role of classroom educators, I assign a Critical *Educational* Autobiography, in which students primarily focus on key experiences and interactions that shaped the development of their academic identity and philosophy of teaching and learning. Additionally, since there is no set format for presenting the critical autobiography, there is also no set format for how to incorporate it, but the "Critical Autobiography Analysis and Reflection Questions" later in this chapter has some common questions to pose to students/participants to help guide them through the process.

For educators aiming to teach for the development of a critical consciousness, the critical autobiography can be used in a number of ways to open dialogue and create opportunities to build important personal connections to ideas and concepts.

- Some educators/facilitators assign it at the beginning of their time with students/participants to gain insight about where their students are in relation to issues of social justice and equity.
- Others assign it at the end to assess how well students/participants apply these social justice and equity lenses to their own lives.
- Still others, like myself, assign it at the beginning, but have students refer to and reflect on it *throughout* the semester, and revisit and revise it at the end of the semester to assess growth and development.

Regardless of how instructors and facilitators choose to incorporate the critical autobiography into the course or professional development, there should be some way of sharing or discussing key takeaways. It is in the dialogue that students begin to build the necessary connections between their experiences and interactions, their personal identity development and how that manifests in their motivations, commitments and engagement with their work and the educators they are and hope to become. Personally, I find that weaving the critical reflection analysis throughout the course, encourages students to find a personal connection to each of the topics we discuss, even if that connection is that they *don't* have any personal experiences with the topic we're discussing because that in and of itself speaks to a certain degree of privilege and ability/freedom to ignore a particular reality.

While my pre- and in-service teachers don't always walk away with drastically different views or differing perspectives on the field and their approach to education, it does often spark important "aha" moments where they begin to understand the ways that certain narratives, identities and ideas are constructed, and the dangers of failing to reflect on them deeply and often. However, it is necessary to assign diverse texts, written about and *from* different perspectives, identities, experiences, and realities, and covering historical and current conditions in order to foster deep critical analysis and discussion.

CRITICAL AUTOBIOGRAPHY ANALYSIS AND REFLECTION QUESTIONS

1. What three words or phrases would you use to describe who you are/want to be *as a classroom educator*? How does that align with *who you are* outside of your role as a classroom educator?
2. Based on your past experiences (both inside and outside of your schooling experiences), what are your beliefs about the *purpose of schooling* and the *role of the educator*?
3. Reflecting on the social, political, and cultural contexts of your schooling experiences, what core *similarities/connections* and *differences/gaps* might exist between you and your students?

NOTE: These are just some sample questions to aid students/participants in the process of thinking about how they position themselves and have been positioned in society and begin to unravel the messages they received about race, ethnicity, gender, ability, intellectual ability, and so on. Questions may be added, removed, or changed as necessary, but the goal is not to lead students/participants to particular understandings, but rather explore what naturally surfaces to serve as a foundation for their understandings throughout the course/sessions.

Speaking of critical analysis and discussion, "Critical Autobiography Analysis and Reflection Questions" has questions for individual analysis and reflection as well as discussion questions for those completing or assigning the critical autobiography with a Professional Learning Community, grade/content team, administrators using it with their faculty, professors with their students or professional development facilitators with their participants. The assignment is also easily adaptable for K–12 educators seeking to learn more about their students' identities, but we'll return to that in Chapter 7 when we talk about student-driven practices.

Conclusion

In this chapter, we explored some of the dialogue around teacher identity development and the ways in which this is intricately woven together with teachers' identities. No matter how hard you try to suppress or ignore it, *who you are* comes with you everywhere you go, including when you stand in front of your students. Our personal identities shape everything from our beliefs about our self-efficacy to do our jobs to how we feel about the intellectual capabilities of our students. As you weave together the threads of your story and journey to who you are, you will find what I am calling your *power cords*. These are the components of yourself, the lessons learned, the resources (people and material), the skills and talents, the wisdom and guidance that you can lean on and into to humanize and transform your practice into what you and your students need. These thick cords often seem unrelated or tangential to your practice, and many times they are spun from the pieces of you that bring the greatest joy or the greatest pain. Your power cords are woven together from the threads of you that you think of when you say I am "unapologetically _____", from the activities that ignite your passions, the people who bring you the purest of joy and love you unconditionally (both alive and ancestral). However, it is not always easy, or desired, for us to lead with our power cords as these are also often tied to the pieces of us that cause us to stick out from rather than fit neatly into society's expectations, leading to a common practice of tucking these threads in or attempting to remove them from our identities and practice altogether. Throughout the remainder of the book you will continue to see commentary and stories from the featured teachers. As you read them, reflect on the power cords that you see coming out in their stories, how they manifest in/through their practice, and also how they help you to identify and emphasize *your* power cords in the continued development and evolution of your teacher identity and practice.

Construct Your Critical Educational Autobiography

If you haven't already, take time to construct your Critical Educational Autobiography. You can complete it in *any* format previously listed, or another format that feels more authentic to you and your identities, both inside and outside of the classroom/your role as an educator. Remember, this is a working document/product, and as you engage with this book, read the narratives from the featured teachers and participate in the reflective activities, you may want to make changes to your autobiography. Come back to it as often as you like as you read, and throughout your journey to and through teaching!

References

Allison, D. C. (2008). Free to be me? Black professors, White institutions. *Journal of Black Studies, 38*(4), 641–662.

Beauboeuf-Lafontant, T. (2002). A womanist experience of caring: Understanding the pedagogy of exemplary Black women teachers. *The Urban Review, 34*, 71–86.

Beauchamp, C., & Thomas, L. (2009). Understanding teacher identity: An overview of issues in the literature and implications for teacher education. *Cambridge Journal of Education, 39*(2), 175–189.

Ingersoll, R., Merrill, E., Stuckey, D., Collins, G. & Harrison, B. (2021). *Seven Trends: The Transformation of the Teaching Force, updated January 2021.* Research Report. Consortium for Policy Research in Education, University of Pennsylvania.

Ladson-Billings, G. (2005). Is the team all right? Diversity and teacher education. *Journal of Teacher Education, 56*(3), 229–234. doi:10.1177/0022487105275917

Olsen, B. (2008). Introducing teacher identity and this volume. *Teacher Education Quarterly*, 3–6.

Schaeffer, K. (2021, December 10). *America's public school teachers are far less racially and ethnically diverse than their students.* Pew Research Center. https://www.pewresearch.org/short-reads/2021/12/10/americas-public-school-teachers-are-far-less-racially-and-ethnically-diverse-than-their-students/

Sealey-Ruiz, Y. (2022). An archaeology of self for our times: Another talk to teachers. *English Journal, 111*(5), 21–26.

Sfard, A., & Prusak, A. (2005). Telling identities: In search of an analytic tool for investigating learning as a culturally shaped activity. *Educational researcher, 34*(4), 14–22.

Welch, S. D. (1990). *A Feminist Ethic of Risk.* Fortress Press.

Chapter 2

Weaving Together Humanizing Narratives

So much of schooling is dominated by the belief that school-based education is the 'way out,' on narrow, often inaccessible, roads to limited views of 'success.' Imagine what roads of possibility would open up if instead of viewing education as a 'way out' we approached it as a 'way in'—into our authentic selves, into deeper truths and more effective solutions, into real freedom of thought/expression, and into new realities.

Instagram Post
@drcourtneyrose (October 10, 2021)

Recently, I listened to a recording of Dr. Wayne Dyer, who was a professor, internationally known speaker, and author in the area of self-development and spiritual growth. In the recording, Dr. Dyer told the story that immediately made me think about some of the dominant enactments of teacher identity that I see within K–12 schools. The story is about four philanthropists who were visiting a village and taken to a prison where a group of conquerors had imprisoned most of the village's men. The first philanthropist was very wealthy and after noticing that the men did not have clean water to drink, offered to donate some of his wages to have a water purification system installed for the prisoners. His offer was honored and he felt as though he had fulfilled his purpose and felt good. The second philanthropist saw that the men were sleeping on rocks and didn't have blankets, so he took his funds and bought blankets and bedding for the people so they could be comfortable when they slept at night. He was also granted this right and he donated his money for this purpose, and just as the first philanthropist, he felt as though he was fulfilling his destiny. The third philanthropist noticed that the food being served was inadequate, just beans, bread, and water. He was a farmer and offered to donate food from his farm to the prison so the imprisoned would have a more nutritious diet, and similar to the first two philanthropists, felt that he was fulfilling his mission for why he was here. However, the fourth philanthropist was a saint, living not at ordinary human awareness but at higher consciousness levels. During the visit he went and found where the keys were, then returned at night and released all of the prisoners. As Dyer states, "this metaphorical story tells us that when we are living at ordinary levels of awareness there is nothing wrong with those who can help us suffer in comfort, and many of us have learned to do and accept that, and say "Alright, as long as I'm comfortable, even if I'm suffering, it's okay. But there are those who have keys, and those keys can open the prisons."

At this point, you're probably asking yourself: "what does this story have to do with education, and how does it apply to our work as educators?" Don't worry, I am not suggesting that we should think of our work as that of saints, although the profession is often spoken of this way—most often when justifying the lower wages, uncomfortable (and sometimes outright toxic) working conditions that many teachers find themselves in. No, the message that resonated with me in Dr. Dyer's story, actually shifts us away from dehumanizing narratives of sainthood that often cloud the role of educators. As educators, when we have a surface-level understanding and awareness, of the narratives, policies, and practices at play within education and society at large, we more easily accept them, advocating for tools and strategies that simply make navigating inequitable and unjust systems more comfortable. Just as with Dyer's philanthropists, I encounter many, often well-intentioned, educators who do a phenomenal job of teaching students how to better navigate the culture of schooling, but do nothing to disrupt dehumanizing policies and practices.

Identifying the Four Philanthropists in Schools

Operating from this surface-level understanding has detrimental impacts on *all* communities, reinforcing reductive views of intelligence and success that are often easily boiled down to performance on uniformed rote tasks and standardized tests. However, the narratives can have the strongest impact in schools serving communities that already face the brunt of the inequities and injustices inherent in both the education system and society at large. These schools, often serving predominantly Black, Brown, and historically disenfranchised and impoverished communities, can attract individuals who, like Dyer's first three philanthropists, are (or appear) well intentioned in their actions, but end up reinforcing and reproducing damaging narratives because of internalized perceptions of these schools and communities. While presented as separate categories/groups for the sake of this book, it should be noted that individuals often occupy more than one group and may move through them depending on their experiences both within and outside of their work as educators.

Therefore, it's also important to remember that *any educator, school, or district leader* can embody and display the beliefs and characteristics of the groups discussed in the following sections of this chapter, *regardless of racial/ethnic, socioeconomic, or educational background.* Dr. Chris Emdin, noted hip-hop scholar, professor, is the author of the book *For White Folks Who Teach in the Hood. . .and the Rest of Y'all Too.* Upon release, the *New York Times* best-seller received critical acclaim for the powerful strategies that it provided the predominantly White teacher workforce to disrupt internalized deficit-based narratives about Black and Brown youth and how to utilize hip-hop cultural artifacts, aesthetics, and practices to authentically engage students in the *creative* processes of teaching and learning. I've had the pleasure of attending many of Dr. Emdin's talks and lectures, especially during the initial release of the book. One of the points that always stood out to me was how he discussed the title and the fact that people often only referred to it as *For White Folks*, but that it was important to remember the. . .*and the Rest of Y'all Too* because *everyone* who grows up in and attends schools in a given society are susceptible to internalizing and enacting harmful beliefs and practices having accepted them as the norm, the way things are and should be.

As you read the following sections, consider some of the narratives you have internalized through your own educational and social experiences, in the various social groups (family, religion, friends, colleagues) and social institutions (K–12 schools, college/grad school, work, church, etc.) that you move through. Reflect on how these narratives not only impacted how you see and engage with others, but how you see and engage with *yourself*, how they shaped the ways you moved through your own schooling and what you valued/prioritized in your pursuit of "success." Finally, reflect on how these narratives may have informed your own practice, from the choice of what types of schools you prefer to teach in and the design and implementation of your instruction, grading and disciplinary policies and practices. In other words, how might some of these narratives inform the ways you show up in your teaching practices, or for pre-service teachers, how you *envision* yourself showing up?

Also, as you read through the descriptions of each identity/mentality/perspective and the damaging deficit-based narratives they potentially reproduce and act from, reflect on some of the underlying complexities (many of which are also included), counter examples, and counter narratives. As author Chimamanda Adichie noted in her viral TedTalk, *The Danger of a Single Story*, "Stories have been used to dispossess and malign. But stories can also be used to empower and to humanize. Stories can break the dignity of a people, but stories can also repair that broken dignity." In each story we can choose to focus on what folks don't have, didn't do, or could/should do better, and the barriers they face, *or* we can choose to focus on what they are doing extremely well, what they've overcome, and how to leverage that to empower and shift toward further progress. As you read the following sections, think about how some of these narratives played out in your own K–12 schooling experiences, how they informed your identity as a student and as an educator, and how thinking about the things you wish people *would* have focused on instead (those power cords that you learned to tuck away) can help you weave together empowering counter narratives and an even stronger vision for your teacher identity.

The Pity Patrol

The first of these groups is what I call the Pity Patrol. Those falling into this category often paint Black, Brown, and other historically disenfranchised communities/populations as *helpless* or operate from the belief that the discriminatory, exclusionary, and inequitable experiences many of these students face as they navigate society and the educational system means they are weaker, less capable, or more fragile than their White and more affluent counterparts. While emerging and evolving research in both culturally relevant pedagogy (CRP) and social emotional learning (SEL) point to the importance of addressing the socioemotional impacts of facing repeated trauma through observed and personal experiences of racism, classism, sexism, homophobia, and so on, this research also points to the fact that, in navigating these daily lived realities, Black and Brown communities have developed unique tools, skills, and understandings that actually manifest into an incredible strength, resilience and ability to succeed.

While claiming a desire to create supportive environments that reduce frustration, these educators often overcompensate resulting in lowered academic and behavioral expectations that actually increase barriers and further limit opportunities to access necessary resources and experiences. Although these educators often spend a lot of time reviewing research and exploring the historical backgrounds of their school and community, they often (mis)use this data to justify their lowered expectations, and whether intentionally or not, locate the root of the continued issues in the students and their communities. Now you may be thinking at this point, the impact of teacher expectations is very well documented, and it goes without saying that if a teacher does not believe or expect their students to be able to master a skill or task or to behave in a manner that shows they even value or desire to engage in the learning process, a decrease in teacher advocacy seems inevitable. However, what makes those operating within the Pity Patrol mentality different, and maybe more detrimental, than those who simply do hold high expectations for their students, is the belief that they are doing what's in the best interest of their students, that pushing them "too hard" would cause further harm.

This was demonstrated in a 2017 study published in the Harvard Educational Review, which unearthed how "caring" and "experienced" educators perpetuated deficit-based narratives and lowered expectations for their students, many of whom were the children of Latiné immigrants. In the study, researchers visited five schools in Texas and showed a film of children engaging in agency-rich activities in which they made decisions, collaborated with each other, discussed a variety of topics, and moved about the classroom freely. In the debrief of the film, researchers were surprised to hear many of the educators communicate that agency-rich activities such as those seen in the video would not work for their students because they lacked the vocabulary necessary to engage in such activities. Specifically, many of the educators pointed to the fact that their students' parents were not able to assist students in their learning because they themselves had limited education and lacked the vocabulary.

Despite the fact that research shows the type of agency-rich approaches and activities reviewed in the video were extremely beneficial to *all* students, particularly those in Pre-K through third grade, many of the participating teachers and administrators leaned instead into a different area of research: the Word Gap. Many educators, especially those working in early childhood, are likely familiar with the 30 Million Word Gap, or the finding that by age three children in families living in high-income communities are exposed to 30 million *more* words than their peers in families living in low-income communities. The findings from this landmark study, conducted in the 1990s by Betty Hart and Todd Risley, have driven the conversation about closing the disparities between those living above and below the poverty line.

However, critics of the study point to the small number of participants (only 42 families), limited amount of data (researchers only spent one hour a month recording adult/child interactions), and structure of the study (a researcher physically sitting in one's home recording and taking notes on their interactions with their child) as shortcomings of the study that may point to deeper nuances rooted in racial and class bias. As a result, subsequent policies and practices often reinforce a narrative that unnecessarily places blame on parents/caregivers, resulting in policies and practices that perpetuate inequities while seeking to change it. In the case of the previously mentioned Texas study, the educators' utilized the language of the "Word Gap" research to justify the use of less sophisticated strategies that failed to position the students as active agents in the learning process.

While well intentioned and often focused on creating supportive learning environments, educators embodying this mentality can, consciously or subconsciously, reinforce and reproduce the following damaging narratives:

- Many students living in impoverished communities or from certain racial, ethnic, or linguistic backgrounds enter schools with large gaps in foundational skills and vocabulary. (Note: this is often rooted in an overgeneralizing and misapplication of research/data such as the previously discussed Word Gap study).
- Parents/caretakers are unable to assist with their children's learning because they did not attain high levels of education themselves.
- Teacher-led, and often hyper-structured, activities are the best way to close "learning gaps."

The Savior Squad

When left unexplored and unaddressed, the Pity Patrol can evolve into (and is sometimes grounded in) the Savior Squad. We see this often in movies that highlight WHITE educators who come into what is portrayed as an unruly, unorganized, and unsafe schooling environment with predominantly Black and Brown students in an impoverished community and *single-handedly* "turn things around" for their students. Prime examples of these Savior films are *Dangerous Minds* starring Michelle Pfeiffer, *Freedom Writers* starring Hillary Swank, and *The Ron Brown Story* starring Matthew Perry. It's also important to note that in these portrayals, the educators of focus often come from *outside* of the education field entirely through a career change in order to do something that allows them to give back or after they were unceremoniously fired or otherwise removed from their original job/career of choice. Both Michelle Pfeiffer and Hillary Swank's characters pursued teaching as they walked away from, or were pushed out of, their prior corporate careers, and with zero experience in the classroom, and were placed in the rooms of students who likely needed the *most* experienced and passionate educators at the helm.

They are also typically positioned in direct opposition to the existing school administration and staff (who are often also people of color) and the students' parents/families—all of whom display a complete lack of care for the children and/or their educational endeavors. Ron Clark, who would become the founder of the large and highly publicized network of charter schools, The Ron Clark Academy, was portrayed as the *sole* advocate for the students in a school and community that had completely written them off. While often lauded as a display of the powerful role an educator can play in students' educational experiences, Savior Squad educators also tend to reinforce and reproduce three false and damaging narratives about impoverished and BIPOC communities:

- These communities do not prioritize education, including the administrators and teachers in the building, many of whom are from the communities themselves.
- Parents/caretakers are largely uninvolved because they are incapable of providing students with the necessary support due to their own limited education *and* they do not desire to be engaged in their children's lives, especially their schooling experiences.
- The solution for "turning things around" and "saving" certain students, communities, and schools requires the involvement of someone who comes in from outside of the community itself.

A counter example to the Savior Squad mentality and identity that is portrayed in the previously mentioned films can be seen in the film *Sister Act 2* starring Whoopi Goldberg. Similar to *Dangerous Minds*, *Freedom Writers*, and *The Ron Clark* story, the students in *Sister Act 2* are initially portrayed as a tough group to manage and generally disengaged from the learning process, and have "run off" multiple music teachers. However, unlike in the other movies, the other nuns in the school recognize that they need to enlist the assistance of someone who both has the necessary skill sets, expertise, and background to not only teach the content, but also build more authentic and affirming learning experiences *with* the students. In doing so, Whoopi's Sister Mary Clarence doesn't come in and dictate to students how to be, but rather taps into and pulls out their natural gifts and talents in a way that not only re-engages them in the learning process, but also transforms the culture and climate of the entire school and church community.

The Bootstraps Crew

The third category is the Bootstraps Crew. This group relies heavily on examples of "success stories" of individuals (either themselves, members of their family/ancestry, or well-known individuals from the population/community they are working in/with) to point to the ways in which circumstances *could* be better if only they worked harder, cared more, stopped making excuses, valued education, and so on. These folks often adamantly refute claims of privilege, whether on racial, social, or gender lines, again citing the hard work of themselves and others as evidence. Leaning into narratives of those who pulled themselves up by their bootstraps and made a way out of nothing, or didn't wait for handouts or someone to come and "save" them, members of the Bootstraps Crew's approach lean into a *myth of meritocracy* that while, on the surface, claims to promote and develop a sense of agency, often completely overlooks the long-standing impacts of historical inequities and injustices that have produced an uneven playing field and left many without boots to begin with. As with the other two categories, this stance reinforces and reproduces the following damaging and deficit-based narratives:

- Everyone has an equitable and fair shot to succeed, and if you are not achieving academic or financial success, then you need to work harder or figure out what you are doing wrong.

- Success is often defined by one's ability to "get out of" or leave their community behind, or be seen as different and exceptional from the other members, further perpetuating the belief that there is nothing of worth in said community, and that it is better to leave than to pour resources into it.

Again, similar to the first three philanthropists in Dyer's story, the members of each of these groups often genuinely feel as though they're operating from *their* greatest good and *for* their students' greatest good. Their efforts appear rooted in desires to help students, particularly those in historically marginalized communities and populations, better navigate schools and society. However, in each of these groups, digging deeper, exploring the historical roots of the education system, and its purpose and function within society, can open opportunities for educators to develop a critical consciousness similar to that of the fourth philanthropist in Dyer's story. From this deeper sense of self and purpose, educators, students, school leaders, and other key stakeholders can collectively identify and access the keys to free each other from the structures that produce the inequities altogether.

PAUSE, REFLECT, DISCUSS: Weaving Together Counter Narratives

1. For each of the perpetuated narratives by those operating through a Pity Party, Savior Squad, or Bootstraps Crew mentality/identity, reflect on the data and observations that may fuel these narratives and make it easy for one to justify them.
2. Then, complicate those responses and think of some counter narratives and examples, including those from your own life and experiences, that can help you weave together a counter narrative for each one.
3. Share and discuss your lists, brainstorming what might change if educators, administrators, and policymakers approached their work from the perspective of the *counter narratives*.

NOTE: This entire activity can be completed individually first with each participant/student developing individual responses to points 1 and 2 and then discussed in groups/professional learning communities followed by a whole group/class discussion, OR the entire activity can be completed in small groups/professional learning communities.

Schooling versus Education

At one point while working on my dissertation, my sponsor/chair started providing feedback and edits at what she called the "word level," pushing me to think about certain words that I chose to refer to different concepts, often with the question "Is this what you mean to say?" or "Are you okay with contributing to the narrative that frames this phenomena or group as such?" Although she never urged me to make a change, but merely just asked a question, this push to think about my individual word choices was admittedly daunting and frustrating at first. However, by the time we made it to the chapter covering my second set of findings, I was incredibly grateful for the process because it forced me to not only engage deeply with my data, but also with *myself*, as I began to realize that changing the *words* we use to talk about something can be a radical act of disruption.

I take this same approach in my courses with my students. I encourage them to reflect on how the words they choose shed light on some of the damaging narratives they've internalized about themselves, others, and processes of teaching/learning. Through this language analysis, my students and I are able to dig into narratives of race, gender, socioeconomic status, diversity, equity, and justice that unearth "coded language" or words that we have all been conditioned to use to make it easier or more palatable to talk about and around the persistent social injustices and inequities that impact various populations both within and outside of schools.

The first narratives we interrogate through language analysis are those around the purpose of schools and education, and whether there is (or should be) a distinction between the two. Each semester, on the first day of classes, I engage my students in the School/Schooling versus Education activity described in the following Visualization Activity. This is the first of many activities designed to complicate ideas and concepts students *thought* had very simple, universal definitions or applications prior to taking the course. Typically, the representations of school/schooling are what you might find if you look up *school* on the internet: school buildings, classrooms with desks in rows facing a board, textbooks for the core subject areas, and so on. What is always most fascinating to me is what students draw for "education." Sometimes these drawings look very similar to the school/schooling drawings with students stating that education is the actual *stuff*, the academic content, that is taught when we go to school. Others draw wildly different representations of each of the words, with education being more of a process that includes, but is not limited to, what is learned in the classroom.

VISUALIZATION ACTIVITY: Schooling versus Education

STEP 1—CREATE: Tell students to draw or create a collage of images that represent SCHOOL/SCHOOLING and a drawing/collage that represents EDUCATION/EDUCATING. Let them know that they must be prepared to explain their visuals and how they reflect/depict the corresponding term.

NOTE: Do not give any further instructions. Students might ask for clarity, but just keep repeating the original prompt of draw school/schooling and education/educating.

STEP 2—GALLERY/SHARE: Either prepare a physical gallery with the SCHOOL/SCHOOLING visuals on one side of the room and the EDUCATION/EDUCATING visuals on the other (you can have students put their explanations near their images in writing, or leave them open to interpretation and have a silent gallery walk) OR have each group share their drawings and explanations one at a time.

STEP 3—REFLECT/DISCUSS: As a group reflect on the similarities and differences between the various representations of each. Try to come to a collective definition of *school/schooling* and *educate/education*, specifically focusing on the purpose of school/schooling as compared to education.

Although *schooling* and *education* are often used interchangeably, many scholars and educators find that they do not represent the same concepts. Education is a process that we are constantly engaging in through every interaction and experience that we have—we learn about ourselves, others, and the world around us. While we acquire an education in schools, the process of being educated is not confined to school buildings and classrooms. Schooling, on the other hand, speaks specifically to the learning that is acquired in the halls and classrooms of K–12 buildings. Some limit schooling to the learning of reading, writing, history, math, and science that takes place through classroom instruction and evaluation practices that often leave out students' unique experiences or leave them unprepared for the critical thought processes necessary to navigate life's unforeseen circumstances. Featured teachers Joscelyn and Jeff speak to the shifts in their thinking that moved them from academic schooling to educating for life.

FEATURED TEACHERS: From Schooling to Education

Joscelyn

If I go back to that, go back to that teacher who started out really confident. . .I was almost overly confident in my ability to go in and get the job done right. I went to Seton Hall. I loved the program, the Education program there. I had a great time, but was not at all prepared to even understand all that my students would come to the table with, and then I was just trying to layer academic content on that and push that aside because I had no training on dealing with any adverse experiences whatsoever. But I got so amped up, so excited to teach, because [my Education program] taught me all these fun and exciting ways to teach academic content but not how to understand the lives of my students so it all fell flat. I couldn't get through a single lesson. The challenges that students were bringing along with them took over every day, and took over any opportunity that I had to grow because I was not in community with anyone else that had the perspective or the time or the will to pour

(continued)

(continued)

into me. In those moments, it was more that I shut the door and said, girl, you'll get through it, I did. I was participating in this legacy of avoidance. It was just what I knew to be true at that time. It's like all teachers went through the fire and you just have to get through the fire, you'll either get through it, or you'll quit and you'll leave, you'll leave it or you won't make it. It was like this is how you see if you got it. But that's not at all the truth. That's not at all the truth because I was leading from a stance of not bringing my full self to the classrooms and not creating a space where my students were bringing their full selves into the classroom either, I had zero community focus at all, and so if I didn't have a community telling me that around me, and I'm just trying to get through every day, when I look back on it, it's like, wow, what kind of experience did those fourth graders, when I started out really have? They were just making it through it and surviving just like I was.

Jeff

Yeah, I think the word *measuring* causes problems because then you have to figure out, well how do you measure it? Obviously, the easiest way to measure anything in schools is by some sort of test score, which is fine. I mean, because obviously, if you're teaching some particular subject, you need to be able to translate those skills over to the students. You want them to grow and develop those particular school skills in that particular subject matter. Great, but my view of teaching is that the subject matter, for me Math, is just the tool for what I'm trying to accomplish because I'm not really trying to make my students great Algebra students, right? I mean, they're going to become great Algebra students as a result of reaching the other goal. The other goal, the real goal, is to use Algebra as a method of teaching them how to think and learn on their own feet for themselves, how they problem solve, deduce everything, and just question and go through a process that is logical to come to some sort of conclusion that they can feel strongly about. That makes sense. And then compare that contrast it, maybe fix it, whatever. So, it's hard to measure that, you know, being successful at that is hard to measure.

That's not going to show up particularly on test scores. Some people can have really high test scores but can't think their way out of a paper bag. But they're graded on regurgitating information. You're gonna have people that, for whatever reason, don't test well, but are really, really bright, intelligent people who can figure things out just anything that you throw at them, they can figure their way out of it. I don't know how to quantify that, but that's the goal. For me, that's the goal, trying to have the students be much better at the end of each year, at thinking on their own, be more confident in themselves and their ability to handle whatever comes along to them. And, like I said, if you do those two things the Algebra is coming. They're gonna know the Algebra. That's the easy part. They'll know that if they do those first few things the algebra's a lock.

Individual Reflection/Collective Discussion

1. Identify the examples of "schooling" versus "education" in Joscelyn and Jeff's comments.
2. Did your own K–12 experiences lean more toward "schooling" or "education"? Explain.
3. Reflecting on and referencing Joscelyn and Jeff's comments, discuss how dominant narratives about intelligence and success might arise from different approaches to teaching and a clear distinction between "academic schooling" and "education for life."

The Historical Role of Schools

Dominant policies and practices utilized within K–12 schooling, in any setting and capacity, often result in one being "schooled" on *much more* than reading, writing, and arithmetic. Researchers within the fields of sociology and anthropology note that schools and the formal curriculum serve as sites and tools through which to communicate dominant beliefs, morals, and values, and many argue that the very process of formal schooling is intended to perpetuate and maintain existing power relations to support existing hierarchies (Althusser, 1971; Shujaa, 1993). Since the inception of the compulsory American schooling system, various laws, mandated policies, curricular designs, and education reform agendas enmeshed in deficit-based constructions of difference and diversity have been used to limit access to educational opportunities and resources for those on the margins of society (Anderson, 1988; Kliebard, 2004; Nasaw, 1979). Historically, constructions of race, gender, (dis)ability, and social class have been used to establish a cultural norm rooted in the ideals of a white, middle-/upper-class, male-dominated society (Delpit, 1988; Gay, 2000; Irizarry, 2009; Ogbu, 1992). Within this framing, perceived social and cultural differences resulted in the continuous labeling of those who deviate from or are not able to fit within the norm as "socially and/or culturally deprived" in ways that can lead to the internalization of narratives that define what, and who, is most valuable, desirable, and meaningful within a given society.

Again, an overview of historical policies and practices show us how, through limiting access to formal schooling and education for some, narratives of intellectual inferiority and social/cultural depravity were created and reinforced. When the initial education reformers began campaigning for a publicly funded school system and compulsory education for all, the biggest resistance came from southern Whites, scared of what would happen if their recently freed Black southerners were now able to obtain a formal education. This sparked many debates over the "proper" education for Black citizens, the most famous of which is the debate between Booker T. Washington and W.E.B. DuBois. Washington, born enslaved, feared that fighting too hard against the racial discrimination of the time could ruin all chances of economic growth for Black people, and instead promoted education in agricultural and crafting skills that would enable Black people to develop the virtues of patience, enterprise, and thrift as they built economic wealth and were able to integrate into society. Conversely, DuBois, born free, argued for a much different approach, arguing that Washington's approach would only perpetuate racial oppression. Instead, DuBois pushed for the identification of the Black community's "most exceptional men," which became referred to as the *Talented Tenth*, who would attend the nation's finest schools and lead the race into better circumstances through their participation in the political and financial sectors of society. While the Washington/DuBois debate remains highly contentious, it still informs many discussions and decisions made in schools today, namely, the push for vocational programs and their values in certain communities over others.

The formal education of other historically marginalized groups faced similar battles. Nearly 20 years before the historic *Brown vs. Board of Education* decision, there was the *Mendez vs. Westminster* decision in which two California families claimed discrimination based on ancestry and language deficiency after they were told their children would have to attend an all-Mexican school, where they focused on teaching domestic and agricultural skills, rather than their local neighborhood school. The *Mendez* case set the precedent for future education discrimination cases, including *Brown*. One of the most egregious uses of schools as sites of creating and perpetuating deficit-based narratives is the Native American Boarding schools that ran in the United States and Canada from the late 19th century to the early 20th century.

Initially, the U.S. Government forced Native American children to attend these schools under the belief that they could be used to "kill the Indian. . .save the man," as stated by Captain R.H. Pratt during a speech given at the National Conference for Charities and Correction. Eventually, Native American families brought their children to the schools on their own because there were no other options. Native American children were separated from their families and cultural ways of knowing and being for extended periods, their long hair cut, their tribal clothing swapped out for more traditional American clothing, and many were punished and beaten for using their home languages.

Consequently, while many would like to say these horrific acts of forced assimilation are a thing of the past, when we critically examine practices and policies of the present, we see similar, albeit less blatantly horrific, acts playing out. For example, recently, numerous stories of Black children being told to cut their hair or wear it in styles that are less "distracting" when they come to school with natural afros, braids, or locs have made headlines, and many of these students were either sent home or refused the opportunity to attend milestone events like graduation if they refused. Additionally, schools and districts with large populations of students for whom English is not their first language often find themselves facing repeated battles for the necessary support, resources, and funding to provide adequate bilingual education to ensure their students have the best chance at succeeding. These practices and policies have historically limited certain students' access to quality formal educational experiences, a hard truth and reality to face on its own. But they also send implicit messages about these students' and their communities' value, worth, and belonging within schools and society that inform how they see, and most importantly, are seen by others, including the educators who stand before them year after year.

Conclusion

As discussed in the previous chapter, the work of educators is often framed as a "calling" with many driven to it to create change for and with their students. However, in fulfilling that calling and "doing the work" of creating change we must understand the narratives that shaped and continue to shape the current realities in which we live and teach. Facing history isn't always easy, but as James Baldwin wrote in a 1982 essay for the *New York Times,* "Not everything that is faced can be changed, but nothing can be changed until it is faced." It is within the stories of our past that we can identify the keys necessary to fully occupy our teacher identities as the fourth philanthropist in Dyer's story and liberate our students, and ourselves, from dehumanizing narratives.

However, recent efforts to limit discussions of these historical and present-day realities and their roots in race-based discriminatory beliefs make it more challenging to identify the keys to create effective learning communities for today's public school students. The intensified political landscape of public school education has created a war-like mentality for many teachers as they constantly face new battles that encroach on their expertise and ability to provide adequate and meaningful education for the incredibly diverse students sitting in today's public schools. In the next chapter, we'll dig into some of these battles and the impacts that they've had on the perceptions of teaching as a whole.

REVISITING CRITICAL AUTOBIOGRAPHIES: Internalized Narratives

Return to your Critical Educational Autobiography, reflect on the following questions, and add the new information to the appropriate sections:

1. Reflecting on your own K–12 experiences, do you think you had more teachers who fell in the *Pity Patrol*, the *Savior Squad*, the *Bootstraps Crew*, or operated more as the fourth philanthropist leaning into liberating practices? How did this shape your schooling experiences?
2. What messages did you internalize about yourself, your intellectual capabilities, your value and sense of belonging within your school and society as you navigated K–12? Identify some key experiences and interactions along that journey.
3. What messages have you internalized, or what are the dominant beliefs and narratives, about YOUR students (or the students you hope to teach)? How do you think this has informed and shaped your practice and vision for yourself as an educator?
4. After reading this chapter, how has your understanding of the role of schools and purpose of the educator changed or deepened?

References

Adichie, C. The danger of a single story [Video]. TED. https://www.ted.com/talks/chimamanda_ngozi_adichie_the_danger_of_a_single_story

Althusser, L. (1971). Ideology and ideological state apparatuses. In *Lenin and philosophy and other essays* (pp. 127–186). New York: Monthly Review Press.

Anderson, J. D. (1988). *The education of blacks in the south, 1860–1935*. United States: The University of North Carolina Press.

Delpit, L. D. (1988). The silenced dialogue: Power and pedagogy in educating other people's children. Harvard Educational Review, 58, 280–298.

Gay, G. (2000). *Culturally responsive teaching: Theory, research, and practice*. New York: Teachers College Press.

Hart, B., & Risley, T. R. (1992). American parenting of language-learning children: Persisting differences in family-child interactions observed in natural home environments. Developmental psychology, 28(6), 1096.

Irizarry, J. G. (2009). Representin': Drawing from hip-hop and urban youth culture to inform teacher education. *Education and Urban Society, 41*(4), 489–515. doi:10.1177/0013124508331154

Kliebard, H. M. (1995). *The struggle for the American curriculum, 1893–1958* (2nd ed.). New York: Routledge.

Kliebard, H. M. (2004). The struggle for the American curriculum, 1893–1958. Psychology Press.

Nasaw, D. (1979). *Schooled to order: A social history of public schooling in the United States.* New York: Oxford University Press.

Ogbu, J. U. (1992). Understanding cultural diversity and learning. *Educational Researcher, 21*(8), 5. doi:10.2307/1176697

Shujaa, M. J. (1993). Education and schooling: You can have one without the other. *Urban Education, 27*(4), 328–351.

Chapter 3

More than a Numbers Game: Recruiting, Retaining, and *Sustaining* Educators

Reminder: "Teacher" is not a monolith. Finding effective solutions for retaining and sustaining teachers requires digging into the ways that identity shapes how one sees and is seen within the role of "teacher" and the structure of "schooling" and the nuances at the root of why so many have chosen to leave.

Tweet/Instagram Post
@drcourtneyrose (October 18, 2022)

During the spring semester of 2020, I was an adjunct professor at the university for which I still currently teach. Now in my fourth semester, well, fifth counting summer 2019, I was beginning to hit my stride with my courses and feeling more comfortable and confident in my new roles as "professor" and "teacher educator." However, about halfway through the semester I walked into my evening section of one of my courses, and before I even got both feet across the threshold, the students began shouting that campus would be closed for the next two weeks. The nation had slowly started grappling with a public health situation, at that time being referred to as the novel coronavirus COVID-19, or more casually Corona or simply "The Rona." Ultimately, it was titled the SARS-CoV-2 and referred to as a pandemic. Universities and K–12 schools/districts across the nation began closing their doors and shifting to remote learning as city and state officials ordered citizens to stay indoors as much as possible indicating that this would "slow the spread" of the virus.

For many, ultimately, that two-week cautionary lock-down turned into over two years of navigating unforeseen and unprecedented circumstances. K–12 educators and school leaders found themselves at the heart of many debates as local, state, and national officials grappled with how to continue to educate and care for students with as little disruption to the natural order of things amid a time that felt anything but natural or normal. With many schools ordered to shut their doors, the switch to remote learning left some students and educators without reliable access to the necessary technology or Wi-Fi services, or the training necessary to adequately utilize them for meaningful instruction. This added a concern, beyond the digital divide (less access to the internet and other forms of technology) that already existed in some communities. Additionally, with a very contentious election and a resurgence of urgency around matters of racial injustice and police brutality in the wake of the murder of George Floyd, the political divides within the country reached a boiling point, leaving everything up for public critique and political/legal scrutiny, including *what* and *how* educators should be teaching.

Schools as "Battle Zones"

According to professional education association Phi Delta Kappa International's 2022 "PDK Poll of the Public Attitudes Toward the Public Schools," 62% of respondents would *not* want their child to choose teaching as a career. Citing concerns about poor pay and benefits, high stress and overly demanding working environments/conditions, personal safety concerns in the wake of increasing reports of school shootings, and a general lack of respect among their primary reasons, many of the respondents reported that while they respect those who take on the role, they simply would not want to see their own child facing the same challenges in their careers (Stanford, 2022). These shifting perspectives on teaching are not only coming from those on the outside of the profession either. At the time of writing this book, the American public school system is facing what many are calling the worst teacher shortage in history. Heading into the 2022–2023 school year, one survey found that nearly three-fourths of responding principals and administrators did not receive enough applicants to fill critical teaching vacancies (Sparks, 2022). My own home state, Florida, reported 4,961 teacher vacancies in the first week of August 2022, which is more than double the number of vacancies heading into the 2021–2022 school year (FEA, 2022).

Additionally, on top of the aforementioned pre-existing issues of low teacher pay and perceived lack of respect for educators, many choosing to leave identified added weight and new pressure on their backs brought on by the conditions of what was deemed a pandemic by public health officials and increased political and social unrest during and after the 2020 Presidential election. Feeling continuously devalued, dehumanized, and unsupported in their efforts to provide students with the educational resources and experiences they deserve, both new and veteran educators reached their breaking points, choosing to leave the profession to better prioritize their own physical, mental, and emotional well-being. In fact, while researching, interviewing, and preparing to write this book, I began to notice how often words associated with "war" are used in reference to policies, practices, and experiences in schools. For example, when discussing the work that educators and administrators do, it is common to hear that they are working "on the front lines" or "in the trenches." This is an especially powerful observation as in war zones, those on the front lines are often the least protected from attack, something that is a daily reality for many educators as displayed in the comments from featured teachers Alexia and Deonna.

FEATURED TEACHERS: Teaching as "Battle"

Alexia

It has been pretty consistent throughout. I think my mindset has become, again, with my journey. And myself. . .I've become more confident in myself. And I think that's where it's like, yeah, I'm going through all of these things, but I don't care now. But before I was trying to be a people pleaser, and do the whole tenure thing, I don't care about that. If you don't want to keep me, then just don't. That is your loss. It's not for all of

(continued)

(continued)

the teachers. I can speak for, you know, my co-teachers. They don't necessarily have to experience the same things. Again, I don't follow what you told me to do, because it's wrong, and now I have to be in a back and forth with you. And that leads to the fact that I applied for curriculum, but now they won't hire me for curriculum. I've spoken out against the bullcrap, and they refuse to hire me. Or just different things in like leadership. If I'm on a leadership team, when I speak out, it's like, I'm being aggressive or I come off too hostile because of the way that I speak or the passion that I have. These are kids, and these are lives that we are responsible for. . .for helping in this process, and then we are causing them harm. That is not okay with me. So, I think, even through the pandemic, and going through the changes for that, and seeing education needs to really shift and we need to be pushing those boundaries. I think, for me, because I am like, "How are you guys just going to go back to the way things were? Things were not even good. What is wrong with y'all?" So, in my mind, it is a constant battle because it is battling basically sanity and insanity [based on] what you are choosing to do. This is wrong, but we are just still going to do it. It is wrong. I guess that is why we are using those terms [associated with war or battles]. Yeah. But it is very strange when you put it like that.

Deonna

When I "freedom dream" about what the future could look like, it does not include this antagonistic relationship between stakeholders. But there is such an antagonistic relationship between stakeholders right now. Post-pandemic it got worse. But you know, it was like that before, to be honest with you, right? It was very much like so many teachers are pitted against parents. Teachers are pitted against administrators. Teachers are pitted against the district or downtown, the main office, whoever the power that be is, right, the superintendent wherever they reside. So many teachers are at war with the students that I hate to say it like that, but that is what it feels like. It very much feels like that every day and that is how they would hype us up before we would start the year because you know as an administrator we would be working over the summer and getting ready for the teachers to arrive and it was very much like gearing up for battle girl. That is what it felt like. I think, unfortunately, that is where we are. Like I said, when I "freedom dream"...it is a collective, it is a community, and that does not happen in a community because the systems are interdependent on each other and they recognize that they need each other to thrive. Right? It is a healthy relationship. It is a healthy ecosystem. Right now, our schools are very, very sick ecosystems, right? They have become incredibly unhealthy. So, I think that is where the war is coming from. There is a perceived scarcity. . .a perceived scarcity because in my view, the scarcity is not there. But any time people experience scarcity, honestly, that is capitalism. That is capitalism and competition. So, we have internalized that.

Individual Reflection/Collective Discussion:

1. What are the core "battles" within schools/the education system that Alexia and Deonna are highlighting? What are the roots of these battles?
2. Reflect on if, and how, you've seen these "battles" play out in schools (either from your own experience as a student or teacher/administrator or your observations as a parent/community member).
3. Deonna mentioned that these "battles" have worsened in the wake of the COVID-19 pandemic. What narratives and conditions may have contributed to this intensifying of the battles? Do you think shifting to a more "communal and collective" mindset as she suggests would have prevented this intensified division between the various stakeholders? Why or why not?

Ultimately, while Alexia and Deonna's comments certainly shed light on the increased intensity of the public health event that ensued, as explored in the previous chapter, educational institutions have served as primary sites of the construction, legitimation, and imposition of dominant narratives and ideologies concerning what is *acceptable*, *truthful*, and *rewardable* and within which to engage in *ideological battles*. Specifically, it is within the highly charged political field and social landscape of K–12 schools, colleges, and universities that many racially, culturally, and linguistically diverse students, educators, and parents often find themselves in daily *cultural combat* as they weave together identities that have been framed as problematic within the culture of schooling (Alim, 2007). Therefore, when attempting to (re)humanize ourselves as educators within an increasingly politically charged system and society, it may be helpful to explore how they impact those who have *always* found themselves bearing the brunt of the load.

The "Invisible Tax"

In response to all of the increased tensions and pressures she was hearing from teachers across the country, Portland-based artist Heidi Ambrose drew an image that she felt reflected the added weights teachers were carrying in the midst of the COVID-19 pandemic. In the image, she drew a teacher who appeared to be a White woman carrying four bags on her back labeled "responsibility for public health," "parents' fears," "personal anxiety," and "no info." The caption for the image, which she posted on Instagram, read: "Thinking of ways to support and love the superheroes that are school teachers, who are trying to do their jobs with countless unknowns. Let me know if you have suggestions!" Two weeks later, she posted a second image. This time it showed a teacher who appeared to be a BIPOC (Black/Indigenous/Person of Color) woman. She also had the four bags that the woman in the previous image carried, except instead of being on her back, she was carrying them on her arm. This is because she already had four bags on her back reading "tone policing," "constantly proving your worth," "racism," and "microaggressions." The caption of this image reads "@woket eachers reached out to me with an excellent grasp of the additional weight that BIPOC teachers carry in this time, and commissioned this illustration. These pictured burdens are definitely not all-inclusive though!"

These images struck me when I initially saw them because they powerfully captured so much of what I personally experienced and witnessed within my own K–12 teaching experiences. They made their way around "Teachergram" (the name given to the community of educators/school leaders who post and engage with teacher and education-focused content on the Instagram app), sparking discussions about the need to have more nuanced dialogue about the experiences of BIPOC educators, which intensified in the midst and wake of the pandemic. Prior to 2020, BIPOC educators have always paid what former U.S. Secretary of Education John King refers to as *the invisible tax*. In a 2016 op-ed written for the *Washington Post*, King notes that although more teachers of color are being hired than ever, they are leaving at much faster and higher rates than their White counterparts, and a key factor is the invisible tax they often pay when they are one of a few in a school building. This tax comes in many forms of unacknowledged and uncompensated labor due to their racial/ethnic identities and the assumption that they are better equipped and prepared to connect and communicate with BIPOC students and families because of their perceived shared experiences For example, BIPOC educators are often tasked with being the key disciplinarians or mentors for BIPOC students, and act as liaisons between the school and BIPOC parents/caretakers.

In today's politically charged climate, BIPOC educators are also disproportionately tasked with leading Diversity, Equity, and Inclusion (DEI) efforts and handling unforeseen equity and diversity issues. This has placed many BIPOC educators in a very precarious position, attempting to carefully navigate what to say, when to say it and how to say it within a climate that is, in many states, not as welcoming to these efforts at this point in time, further placing additional pressures as they try to balance that load. Learning to navigate these taxing circumstances is one of the key factors leading to the tensions and battles expressed by featured teachers Alexia and Deonna. However, research also shows that they lead to quicker levels of burnout, and the lack of attention to addressing these circumstances or framing of teachers who raise these issues as problematic can sometimes lead to silencing that extends well beyond the walls of classrooms, deeply impacting teachers' sense of self and agency, as reflected in the comments from featured teacher Diedra.

FEATURED TEACHER: Dimming Your Light

Diedra

I was also in a space where there was predominantly White leadership making decisions for predominantly Black students. I am a Black woman who has more leadership, more experience period, than all of them. Instead of it being seen as an asset, it was being seen as a threat. This is what I tell educators all the time. Those things impact you. You can be as confident as possible, you can be strong, all those things, but when you're entering spaces where you don't feel valued, or you don't feel like what you're bringing to the table is important, even though you know it is, that can impact you. For me, I would see my students who looked like myself, they looked like me. They looked like they could be my nieces and nephews and cousins, and then when I would see what would happen in the school, and then see, like, the fact that I felt powerless when I would try to advocate for them. But instead of that working, it ends up that, I'm the bad person now because I've spoken up. So, what happens in situations like that, often, is we start to silence ourselves when we start to feel like okay, maybe I need to just—maybe it's not worth it, maybe I need like, you know. . .we just doubt everything. I believe that carries over into our personal lives, where we start to lose our voice to a certain extent. You know, that can happen in relationships, or in just any situation. We spend so much time in schools. So, if you're in a school where you are constantly not feeling like your voice is valid, or you're important, and all of those things, how could we not expect that to seep into just who we are as a person? So there's a lot of—there's a lot of like unlearning that has to happen when you finally remove yourself from that situation, because even when I went to a different school, and I had previously been at like a toxic school, and I went to a new school that didn't seem as toxic, I was silencing myself. I was not really socializing with the other employees, I was just like, "I'm here, I'm leaving because I just didn't want any drama." I didn't want drama. I did not want it. So, I didn't share my expertise. People were surprised. They did not know I had all the expertise that I had. They are like, "Oh, my gosh, you used to do that?" And I am like, "Yeah, I did." But you know, it is not a big deal. But, I had already just dimmed my light to the point from that previous experience that I was bringing it into this new one.

Individual Reflection/Collective Discussion

How does Diedra's commentary shed light on the "invisible tax" that many BIPOC educators pay in their work in public schools?

Research also shows that the *invisible tax* is felt differently based on the unique intersections of identities that educators hold. For example, Black men, who comprise only 2% of the teaching population, find that the invisible tax has an especially detrimental impact on their ability to focus on their instructional practice. Even when in schools with high numbers of BIPOC educators, they are often one of a few, if not the only, Black males in an instructional position. Thus, they find themselves spending a large portion of their planning or non-instructional time mentoring or handling behavioral and academic issues that arise with Black boys in the school. This additional tax, combined with the previously discussed narratives about teaching as a profession, and the political tensions around *what* and *how* classroom educators can/should do their jobs, has not only pushed BIPOC educators out of the classroom, but has been one of the key factors in the continued lack of Black men in the classroom. Featured teachers Jeff, Bobby, and Brian, all identifying as Black men, speak directly to their views on being a part of "the 2%," what fuels it, how they've navigated it, and their advice on how to better recruit and retain Black male educators.

FEATURE TEACHERS: The 2%

Jeff

I think it is that a lot of career choices that students make or young people make are just based on their experience and their observations. And so for me, I never thought about teaching because I went through my

(continued)

(continued)

entire secondary school experience, from kindergarten, through graduating high school, never having had a Black male teacher in any subject. Never, and I only know of one. He was a PE [physical education] teacher. All the other people, like you said, were predominantly white women with some white men sprinkled in. And so, it just was not a career that I had any interest in, because my people don't do that, you know, people that's no Black guys doing that. I saw, you know, Black males doing a variety of other jobs, and so I just leaned towards those. As far as trying to entice more black men into teaching, you know, I think you have to be able to find the kind of guys first of all, the kind of people who understand and embrace the actual work involved in this profession. Because it is a professional teaching profession, I think it is an art like anything else. You have to develop a skill base and practice it and improve it and do all those things. I think there is a general thought in society that teaching is easy. School goes from eight to three, you're off for the summer, and you don't really do any work. I thought that, I cannot even lie. When I want to change careers. I was thinking this is probably gonna be a lot easier than what I was doing before, working 60 and 70 hours a week. It is the hardest job I have ever done. To do well, it is really, really hard. But it is also really rewarding because you get to help young people grow and develop their minds and their thoughts. Yeah, that is the other thing. What kind of pushed me and linked me into teaching in the end, and this is how they can connect with more Black males, is that it became a way where I could pay people back. Even though, for me, they weren't Black males, they were not. But there were a handful of really key people in my life, outside of my family, who had played a critical role in helping me become the person I am now. They believed in me, they treated me really well, they demanded a lot of me and they expected a lot of me. They expected more of me than I thought I had, and they told me the truth. They wouldn't let me settle for anything less than my best. They helped create the person that I am now. So, doing this now, I'm just trying to repay them through whatever I can do. If I can do the same thing for students who I have now, then that's the best way for me to repay those people. I think if we framed it that way, like, hey, you know, you guys made it, you guys became successful, because of at least a handful of people in your educational career. This is where you can do the same thing for, you know, some young people.

Bobby

I think the problem starts very early. How often are Black boys in particular told "You can be a teacher"? If anything, the expertise and the genius of Black boys. . .they're primarily seen through what they can do athletically, and so even when you break down that number, even more Black men in STEM, right? A lot of the Black male teachers whom I have witnessed, because I only had two Black women teachers, and I've never had a Black male actually teach me. I've had Black coaches. Wow, I have never had a Black male teacher. Wow. And primarily, that is because they were all gym teachers. And so, you know, they divided the alphabet up, and I had "M" and I never got them. That is just kind of how that worked out. But there is a notion to which if we would feel the genius of Black boys, if we learned how to actually teach, which is part of the [problem], you know, for me, this is like my wheelhouse, because it is part of the work that I do. If we taught Black boys, for example, math in a culturally responsive manner, where they could actually see themselves as mathematicians. . .that is a goal. I want [them] to think of math as a tool for change out there.

Brian

One of the things that I received was this raising by a village of other Black men. These men were from different aspects of my life, right? Some were at school some were at church, some were part of organizations that I was a part of, some were in my family. I think one of the things that we perhaps have to think about is, does that village of men have to exist just in an educational space, or are there other spaces for those men to show

(continued)

(continued)

up and to pour into other young men? When I think about what were those other spaces? It was because I was a part of a rites of passage program that wasn't connected to my school. It was because I was a part of a church organization that had youth groups, and then the youth group was even segmented into just an all males youth program. So, I think, in a real sense, some of those programs no longer exist. We haven't maybe poured into some of those mentoring programs, or some of those church programs, or some of those other organizations that will help to pour into Black boys? Right? And I think that is one of the reasons why we see just 2% of Black men that exist in an education space. Society in a real sense, seeks to erase the power of men in the lives of children of black men and the lives of children. And they seek to erase it in a variety of ways. One of the resources and opportunities there are for men to be in educational spaces, right? When they are in educational spaces, it's so hard for them to stay for a variety of reasons, right? They are looked at as being just the disciplinarian. Or they are forced to do certain things that maybe other educators do not have to do. And so many of them are pushed out by design. Our children do not have an opportunity to see examples of themselves, they do not have an opportunity to glean from people that look like them. And so, I think there is a systemic issue that we also have to address. . . .

Individual Reflection/Collective Discussion

1. Jeff, Bobby, and Brian's comments all speak to some of the dominant narratives and factors impacting Black men's pursuit of teaching as a career. What do you see coming through in their commentary/reflections?
2. Considering the comments of Jeff, Bobby, and Brian, what are some suggestions for key areas to address the recruitment and retention of Black male educators? What are some new or different questions that those in power should be asking?

Weaving Together Supportive Learning Communities

Exploring the unique experiences of BIPOC educators, points to the need for more nuanced approaches to recruitment and retention practices that not only encourage BIPOC educators to enter classrooms, but also support and *sustain* them so that they stay. Scholar and author Gloria Ladson-Billings (2022) notes that when she presented on the excellent pedagogical practices of the successful teachers of African American students in her groundbreaking work *The Dreamkeepers*, a common reaction from educators and schools was "well that's just good teaching." In her work, Ladson-Billings affirms these remarks arguing that the culturally relevant practices enacted and embodied by the educators in her study were central to transformative and successful learning experiences for Black children *and* other students who have been historically under-served within our nation's public schools. Similarly, I argue that, since its inception, our public school system has not always done the best job of supporting educators, particularly those who experience the brunt of the weight, who have always carried additional baggage, or paid additional emotional and physical taxes. Therefore, looking to research that focuses on more nuanced approaches to recruiting, retaining, and *sustaining* BIPOC educators can lead us to more effective approaches and strategies that will better recruit, retain, and *sustain* all educators.

Critical Reflection and Analysis

Dr. Micia Mosely, educator and founder of the Black Teachers Project, an organization designed to support the shrinking population of Black educators, is often approached by school/district leaders seeking to recruit and hire Black educators. In a recent interview, Dr. Mosely stated that although people are usually thrown off, her first step in the process is to ask "Why do you want Black teachers?" Some might scoff at this question or view it as counter-productive to the goal of diversifying the teacher workforce.

However, as Dr. Mosely points out, there *is* such a thing as hiring for the wrong reasons. While research links the presence of BIPOC educators to increased academic performance among BIPOC students, the development of more welcoming learning environments, higher reports of belonging among *all* students, and higher ratings of instructional capabilities from their students (regardless of racial/ethnic background), BIPOC educators are often under-supported, under-developed, overworked, and quickly burnt out as districts recruit to boost diversity numbers and attend more to non-instructional needs (i.e., discipline and DEI-related issues/efforts). Reflecting on whether you truly believe in the value and necessity of having more BIPOC educators can help schools/districts/states to build the proper infrastructure to better support and develop them, which in turn, will likely create a better system and structure of support and development for *all* teachers.

Additionally, taking a moment to reflect on the reasons why your school or district could benefit from having more BIPOC educators can lead to a similar type of excavation that Yolanda Sealey-Ruiz pushes for in her archeology of the self, discussed in Chapter 1, by asking how the issues live in your district or school. No issue manifests the same way in each community, which is why no single approach is ever going to work universally. Oftentimes school, district, and state leaders attempt to enact recruitment and retention efforts that meet a current immediate need but do little to address the historical root causes, and ultimately, only provide temporary relief. However, engaging with educators, particularly those whose identities lie at the intersections of historically marginalized populations, might help to pinpoint exactly what needs are being unmet and involve teachers in the process of identifying solutions that actually create supportive and sustaining working conditions.

Collaborative and Collective Efforts

A second area of focus in providing additional support for all teachers, but especially BIPOC educators, is to focus on developing more opportunities for meaningful collaboration and collective action between key stakeholders. One of the most surprising things I learned during my first few years of teaching is how lonely and isolating the job can feel. As a student, I had always seen teachers talking and laughing with each other and assumed that they worked together often, and perhaps in some cases, this was true considering a lot of the schools I attended implemented project-based learning models that required cross-curricular approaches, which I will talk about more later in the book. However, so much of what I learned within my own teacher education program and what I felt when teaching was that once the door to my classroom closed I was really on my own and I often felt very unprepared for the realities in which I was working and teaching.

Professional Learning Communities often provide teachers with the structure to begin forming these collaborative relationships. The typical formations of PLC groups by either grade level or content area taught are designed to encourage educators to collectively identify more effective instructional strategies to meet a specific need for students. When this type of collaboration is woven into the culture, climate, and overall fabric of the school/district community they can be quite effective. Although my first year of teaching was overall a very tough circumstance to navigate, the teachers in the building did come together in really powerful ways. In particular, the fifth-grade team that I worked on worked together from the very first day of school. We not only met as a whole grade level team, but also formed subgroups with the math/science teachers and English/Language Arts teachers meeting to address the specific issues we were having in our content areas.

When it came time to prepare for the upcoming state test, we worked together as a grade-level team to organize the entire fifth grade into intervention groups that were not only based on the content area they needed some more targeted attention in, but also the specific teacher that might provide instruction in the most effective way for that particular student. This required that we not only learn and discuss *our* individual strengths, but that we also spend time learning and knowing our students so we could match them with the best intervention assignment. In addition to *all* of this, we also supported each other with our grade-level disciplinary plans.

We partnered to send students to different rooms when time in another space was necessary for a bit of a cooling off or reflective period, and similar to the academic intervention plan, we noted that certain students connected with and felt more comfortable with teachers on the team other than whom they were assigned to, and that person would often speak to the student if an issue occurred.

Similar things were happening on other grade-level teams, and while it may seem like a lot of additional work, it actually helped to make the often-stressful climate we were navigating feel a bit more manageable. We observed each other, we shared the responsibility of developing lessons and instructional materials, we knew each other's strengths and areas for growth and we supported each other in each of those areas. In the end, the efforts we put into developing this collaborative group opened the walls of our classroom, created a more dynamic and supportive learning experience for our students, and actually freed up time as we split the work load. Within our team, there was no comparison or competition. We were one unit and we moved that way to the best of our ability. When I was called into the office and let go, I went to Ms. Fowler's room (she was our grade-level team leader) and she hugged me as I cried and then gave me a talk that helped me gather myself to go stand in front of my students with my head held high. Even as we all moved on to different schools, we kept in touch, supporting each other from afar for years. I honestly credit that team for helping me to find who I am and who I want to be in this field, and while some have gotten close, I've never found a group that moved as collectively as that group.

Building on this notion of collaboration, many districts and states have started to focus on fostering better relationships between K–12 schools and universities. One approach is the development of "Grow Your Own" programs are designed to recruit future teachers from their own student population who may be more invested in, knowledgeable about, and equipped to create effective learning experiences that meet the specific needs of the students and community. Additionally, stronger district/university partnerships could help to ensure that university-based programs are better able to provide effective educators who feel adequately prepared for the realities of the schools and communities they plan to work for and with. Some university programs look to current K–12 educators and school leaders to serve as part-time adjunct faculty to cover courses in their teacher education and school leadership programs. These educators are often extremely valuable assets to the university-based programs as they are able to provide relevant, firsthand examples of some of the present-day issues and realities of working in schools. For example, in a meeting with some district school leaders who also taught as adjunct professors in the Educational Leadership program at the local university, one individual mentioned that the course they teach often aligns with the time of year where he has to put together the budget for the upcoming school year. He is able to use that process as a teaching tool in the course and actually walk students through it step-by-step so that they can see how it actually pans out in real time, and discuss how to navigate through some of the issues that pop up in the process. Schools and districts seeking to diversify and better support their teacher pool should also look to organizations like the Black Teachers Project whose primary mission is to build collaborative and collective spaces for personal healing, professional development, and community support.

Greater Attention to School Leadership

Finally, this one is a bit more focused on those reading this who are currently in or pursuing leadership roles. It is highly documented that teachers are a primary factor in the quality of the educational experiences and subsequent outcomes that a student is likely to have. Given that they often spend the most time with students during their K–12 academic journeys and lead in fostering the development of the class climate and culture in which learning occurs, it is no surprise that addressing teacher attitudes and effectiveness is a key factor in evaluating student performance and outcomes. As we explored in Chapter 2, the narratives that educators internalize play a major part in shaping the practices they enact with students. Likewise, the narratives that school, and district, leaders hold about their teachers as well as the schools and communities they serve, similarly impact and shape the policies, practices, and subsequent working environments they develop. In many of the surveys exploring why teachers leave, lack of administrative support continuously surfaced as one of the primary reasons. Therefore, districts seeking to provide more supportive and *sustaining* environments should ensure that they are also attending to diversifying and providing continued support and opportunities for professional development to prepare a *school leadership* pool that is prepared to meet the needs of today's teachers, students, and communities.

Conclusion

In this chapter, we explored some of the issues that impact educators' abilities to engage in the work and present barriers to enacting their teacher identities in the ways they may have hoped or envisioned themselves doing. Both visible and invisible taxes have often encouraged educators to pursue ways to apply their skills differently. Again, creating supportive, affirming, and humanizing environments for students *requires* that equal attention is given to providing supportive, affirming, and humanizing environments for educators. There are many important lessons to be learned from those who leave, and in some cases, leaving the classroom to find spaces that create room and support you in doing the work as you know it should be done is the most powerful way to enact your practice. However, there are also many powerful lessons that we can learn from those who choose to stay, often referred to as veteran educators, and in the next chapter, we will dig into some of the intergenerational perspectives and narratives that are often woven together from, by, and about those holding this particular identity.

REVISITING THE CRITICAL EDUCATIONAL AUTOBIOGRAPHY: Sustaining Yourself

Return to your Critical Educational Autobiography, reflect on the following questions, and add the new information to the appropriate sections:

1. Reflecting on this chapter, what, in your opinion, are some of the most pressing issues impacting teachers' abilities to "do the work" of teaching in today's schools and social/political climate? For those currently in the classroom, how have you navigated these new, or more intensified, issues?
2. After reading this chapter, and reflecting on your own experiences/ observations, what advice would you give to schools/districts on how to best recruit, retain, and sustain a diverse teacher workforce?
3. People often tell teachers to stay connected to their "why" or remember that they are "doing this for the kids" as reasons to stay in unsupportive, unsatisfying, and sometimes, unsafe working conditions. How do you respond to these statements? What specific supports and/or resources do you think teachers, or you specifically, need to sustain themselves (yourself) and provide the educational experiences students deserve?

References

Alim, S. H. (2007). Critical hip-hop language pedagogies: Combat, consciousness, and the cultural politics of communication. *Journal of Language, Identity, and Education*, *6*(2), 161–176.

Florida Education Association (FEA). (2022, September). Teacher and staff shortage. https://feaweb.org/issues-action/teacher-and-staff-shortage/

King, J. (2016, May 15). The invisible tax on teachers of color. *The Washington Post*. https://www.washingtonpost.com/opinions/the-invisible-tax-on-black-teachers/2016/05/15/6b7bea06-16f7-11e6-aa55-670cabef46e0_story.html

Ladson-Billings, G. (1995). But that's just good teaching! The case for culturally relevant pedagogy. *Theory into Practice, 34*(3), 159–165.

Ladson-Billings, G. (2022). *The dreamkeepers: Successful teachers of African American children*. John Wiley & Sons.

Sealey-Ruiz, Y. (2022). An archaeology of self for our times: Another talk to teachers. *English Journal, 111*(5), 21–26.

Sparks, S.D. (2022, September 27). What school staff shortages look like now. *EducationWeek*. https://www.edweek.org/leadership/what-school-staffing-shortages-look-like-now/2022/09

Stanford (2022, August 25). Most parents don't want their kids to become teachers, poll finds. *EducationWeek*. https://www.edweek.org/teaching-learning/most-parents-dont-want-their-kids-to become-teachers-poll-finds/2022/08

Chapter 4

Weaving Together Intergenerational Perspectives

> *In most schools there is one person who's been there for YEARS and is the heart & soul of the school community. They've watched families guide one child after another through the halls & maybe even crossed GENERATIONS with some. We are not tapping into their WISDOM enough.*
>
> Instagram Post
> @drcourtneyrose (July 26, 2022)

In December 2021, a scripted television show, *Abbott Elementary*, premiered, depicting the experiences of teachers working in a Philadelphia public school serving predominantly Black students. Using the popular mockumentary format, *Abbot Elementary* attempts to comically yet realistically depict the realities that teachers face when working in these communities by following the daily functioning of the school through five teachers, all at different stages in their teaching careers, the school's principal (whose qualifications for the job are questionable at best), and the janitor who has been at the school for decades. Since its premiere, *Abbott Elementary* received praise from educators across the country for humanizing teachers and the profession itself through explorations of the characters' lives (both inside and outside of the classroom); debunking false narratives about "lazy," "ineffective" educators through stories that display the deep passions and commitments to their students; and accurately portraying the barriers and challenges to providing the educational environments and experiences their students need and deserve.

The show primarily focuses on Janine (played by writer, actor, and show creator Quinta Brunson), an extremely optimistic second-grade teacher in the early years of her teaching career, and the impassioned, and occasionally misguided, approach she takes to help the lives of her students. As we follow Janine and the other teachers in the building we get a unique view of schooling through the eyes, experiences, and identities of the *educators* in the building. Where most shows that take us into school buildings provide insight into how students experience the culture of schooling, *Abbott* is one of the few that spends the large majority of its time exploring the social dynamics that often impact various aspects of teachers' practice and professional development. Most notable is the way that *Abbott* explores the complexities of the perception of and dynamic between new and veteran educators, particularly through its portrayal of one of its more senior educators, Barbara Howard (portrayed by actress Sheryl Lee Ralph).

PAUSE, REFLECT, DISCUSS

Abbott Elementary portrays just about every educator archetype through their main characters: Janine, Barbara, Melissa, Gregory, and Jacob. Watch a few episodes or clips (many clips are available online for free) and reflect on the following:

1. Which *Abbott Elementary* educator(s) do you most closely identify with and why?
2. Which educator(s) do you *aspire* to be more like and why?
3. Reflect on how your responses shed light on your own educational experiences and your conceptualization of the role of the educator or what it means to be an effective educator.

Veteran educators, typically defined by the number of years they have taught (which varies with some naming those in their second decade of teaching and others reserving it for those in their third or fourth decades), can often be painted as having lost their passion, jaded, and exhausted by the almost daily challenges and shifting expectations placed on educators and stuck in their "old school" ways of doing things that pose challenges to some of the recent shifts in approaches to teaching and learning, such as the incorporation of more technology into instructional and assessment practices. Barbara Howard's character certainly leans into some aspects of this perception of veteran educators. For example, in one episode she does not want to let on that she is struggling with the new reading assessment software and accidentally submits data that suggests her kindergarten students are now performing at a much higher reading level. However, what resonates most is the way that Barbara serves as a powerful, wise, nurturing mentor to the new teachers, offering (sometimes begrudgingly) her advice on how to effectively communicate with parents in the community, resolve conflict between students, and structure the instructional day so that learning still remains fun while working within (and around) district and state demands. Through Barbara Howard's character, *Abbott* sheds light on the powerful threads that veteran educators weave between the school and the community, between "old school" and "new school" approaches to teaching and learning, and between our roles as educators and our humanity. In this chapter, we explore the complex narratives that are often woven about veteran educators and the lessons we can learn from the wisdom of those who stay.

Learning from Those Who Stay

As explored in Chapter 3 on the teacher shortage, attention has been focused on what is going wrong in schools and education, what makes teachers leave and how to attract new teachers to the field. While these are all important and necessary questions, they are rooted in a deficit framing of schools and teachers that can breed a sense of hopelessness and helplessness within and around the profession. Shifting focus from the *movers* and *leavers* to the *stayers*, to use language from the National Center for Educational Statistics' (2022) ongoing research on teacher attrition and retention, we can move from a deficit-based lens of "what is making teachers leave" to an asset-based framing that instead asks "what fuels teachers to stay" that may produce more fruitful lessons and solutions.

Models for "Making It Through"

When I was in second grade, my family moved from New York to my dad's hometown in Connecticut. I was so excited to move into the house where we'd spent so many beautiful days and nights filled with family and to have my paternal grandparents living right next door (they moved into my great-grandparents' home). After spending an incredible summer getting acclimated to our new, yet familiar, surroundings it was time to start school that fall. I don't remember much about the details of that first day, but I do remember that when my mom dropped me off with my teacher and headed down to take my brother to his class, it was his *first* first day of school, the teacher paraded me around to various teachers and employees in the building shouting "This is Courtney ROSE. She's Jeff's DAUGHTER and Tina's GRANDDAUGHTER! Can you believe it?" See, not only did we move to my dad's hometown and live in his childhood home, but we also attended the same elementary school he'd gone to as a child and my grandmother previously worked in the cafeteria. Many of the teachers, administrators, and staff either worked there when my dad was a student or during the time after my dad moved on to junior high, but my grandmother remained. Again, I don't remember much about the details of that day, but I do remember that every bit of nerves and anxiety that I'd felt about starting a new grade in a new school and a new city immediately disappeared. I felt connected with the space in a deeply familial way, and instantly felt like I belonged there.

To me, the ability to bridge the past with the present, to connect generations, to bring a sense of familiarity and belonging to an educational space is one of the strongest power cords woven into the identities of veteran teachers and employees in a school building. These teachers, who have often spent their entire careers in the same school (or at least the same district) have seen generation after generation walk the halls. They have witnessed, firsthand, the social and political dynamics impacting the school and its surrounding communities. Often, but not always, these teachers and staff grew up in the community themselves and have strong personal ties and deep personal experience with the daily lived realities of the students and families the school serves. They have been in the profession, watching as wave after wave of policies dictated what they could and should do in their classrooms, navigating shifting perceptions of the role, purpose, and effectiveness of America's schools and educators. Featured teacher and school principal Tanesha reflects on a similar sentiment as she recalls advice from her mentor and the impacts veteran educators can have on a school community.

FEATURED TEACHER: Staying "Long Enough"

Tanesha

Like when I think about staying in education for a long time, like, my mentor told me when I was in my first year teaching, she says, "If you stay long enough, you'll start to see things come back around." We're there. It's coming back around. We need somebody who's willing to actually just stay. I think about teachers staying, social workers staying. People talk [negatively] about veteran teachers all the time, I don't know why they get such a bad reputation. If I could find five veteran teachers right now I would take all their baggage right now. Come on, come on. There's so much to be said about school communities when people stay and see things out, I think that it's really hard to refine your practice if you do it once and you're out.

Growing up, my mother would often repeat one of my grandmother's many sayings: *there's nothing new under the sun*. Although the terms and the specifics may change, the roots of the issues impacting many schools, educators, and the communities they serve remain the same. The advice featured teacher and administrator Tanesha received from her mentor leans into this sentiment as well. Educators who *stay* have not only faced, but *made it through* similar issues and circumstances that present challenges and barriers within the present-day realities within society and schools.

In this regard, veteran teachers not only show newer generations of educators that it is possible to make it through, but also provide models for *how* to make it through. Woven into their teacher identities are the stories of battles won and lost in the name of creating better learning communities and experiences for their students both inside and outside of the classroom while defending their expertise, position, and value within schools and society.

Rooted in Self

The resilience and commitment demonstrated by veteran educators is often rooted in their passion for the work, the love for their students, leaning into similar narratives of "martyrdom" or "answering callings" used to vilify those who choose, or are pushed, to leave (Cohen, 2009; Day & Gu, 2009). However, digging deeper into the personal narratives *from* those who stayed exposes much stronger commitments to and love of *self*. Featured teacher Vennieta, who was in her 21st year as an educator at the time of her interview, touches on this as she reflected on the complexities of taking on, or being given, the title and identity of "veteran teacher."

FEATURE TEACHER: Taking on the "Veteran Teacher" Identity

Vennieta

I'm nine years from retirement, and that number is so weird to me and surreal to be that close. I think that is where I am like, maybe I am a "veteran" because we are talking about retirement. But I have no intention of not retiring in that classroom. I love it. I often find my escape in the lesson plan, you know what I mean? This is a weird space that I am in, but I will be watching TV and realize I am dreaming of some lesson. It took me 20 years to realize I am a very creative person and [curriculum design and teaching] is a creative outlet for me. For example, there is this particular social justice issue that I am passionate about and I heard a Kendrick Lamar song last night, and I cannot stop thinking of all the parallels I can make, and how I can teach my class tomorrow. Sometimes I go to bed thinking about my student who is dealing with a major mental health issue and what we can do to help her. It is just like, I can't find more purposeful work. So, again, the "veteran teacher" thing is one that comes with a huge responsibility, and I am just going to let "veteran" equate to time served, you know, you are up there—time served. But, again, there is a responsibility that veterans just have, which is to say things that other people cannot say, with wisdom.

Importantly, as Vennieta communicates, it is through her role as an educator that she finds a meaningful and purposeful outlet through which to release her creativity and engage in the social justice work that fuels and sustains her. Although her love and passion for her students remains a clear throughline, the degree to which she is able to see and insert *herself* into her work is what continues to sustain and fuel her commitment, even as she acknowledges the damage the system can and has done to so many who find joy and themselves within it. This complex relationship with the education system shows up as an equally complex relationship with Vennieta's, and many other veteran educators' identity as one who stayed, particularly as one who stayed in a district facing the worst of what the system has to offer.

In my research for this chapter, one study stood out to me as particularly intriguing in its framing of the commitments to self that fuel many veteran educators. Exploring the experiences of two Black male educators who each stayed in the profession for over 25 years, Rosetta Marantz Cohen (2009) identifies three primary traits that support longevity and long-term engagement among urban educators: psychological hardiness, narcissism, and an all-consuming love for their subject area. All three of these traits are used to frame the two veteran teachers of focus as operating in opposition to the student-centered, flexible, innovative mindsets encouraged by recent frameworks of "good teaching." As I read the piece I found myself struck by Cohen's framing of the teachers' practice being rooted in a sort of narcissism, seeing it instead as a similar commitment to being one's full and truest self in the classroom.

Too often, in an effort to be "good" teachers, many educators attempt to perform teaching styles and practices they've seen enacted by others or read about in their teacher education courses. While models can provide insight into useful tools and strategies, this tendency to "perform" teaching often leaves some educators constantly playing a character that runs counter to who they are, leading them on the fast-track to job dissatisfaction and burnout. What Cohen's teachers and our own featured teacher Vennieta share in their more seasoned approaches is a realization that meaningful and effective teaching requires teachers to come in their full authenticity. As one of the teachers in Cohen's study shares, if they were to take on some of these other strategies, to play a role within the classroom that felt like inauthentic to who he was, then that would trickle down to the students.

Now I know some of you might be thinking this is the same type of resistance that many educators take about bringing in various culturally relevant or sustaining practices. To that I say, you're right, but that in both cases this resistance to change may be connected to a feeling that to take on these practices would be an inauthentic performance. What many students connect to in an educator's practice, what makes a space *feel* free and open for folks to *be*, to take risks, to feel supported, is that *everyone* in the space is coming as they are, *starting with the educator*. Going back to my first year as a Lead Teacher, I remember struggling to make a strong connection with my students, for some reason the more I tried to build relationships, the more disconnected from them I felt. It took me a while, and a few observations of other educators in the building, to realize that I'd come in playing the part of the teacher I *thought* I was supposed to be rather than bringing the person I *was* into the room, and the students could feel it. Then, to make things worse, when I tried to switch things up I overcorrected, enacting some of the overly restrictive practices I'd seen from teachers in my own K–12 schooling.

If there is one thing that I have learned and seen from some of the best educators, especially veterans in the field, it is this unwavering commitment to being who they are, weaving a thread that seamlessly connected who they are (their passions, commitments, speech patterns, interests, etc.) into their teaching. If more teachers stopped trying to fit themselves into school settings that forced them to change, hide, or otherwise perform teaching in ways that caused misalignment with who they are, then more educators would work in environments where they could make the best impact for students, where they themselves feel supported and valued, and by extension, create environments that enabled students to do and feel the same.

Think about the teachers who constantly have classrooms filled with students during lunch or other down times, the teachers whom students go to for advice, the teachers whom students vote for as their favorite. In many cases, these are those long-standing individuals who "don't play" and "give it to them straight." Students don't have to guess with these teachers because they know who they are and they know who they are going to get day in and day out. What some might read as narcissism is simply a rootedness in self that feels jarring because so many of us have been conditioned to be anything but self. However, to sustain the often unpredictable and overwhelming working environments in which many educators find themselves, it is this rootedness in self that keeps people grounded in their commitments and to their purpose.

Creating Climates Rooted in Systems of Support. . .and Protection

This imagery of a grounded plant or tree came to mind often as I reflected on the wisdom of veteran educators, particularly as I processed some of the additional thoughts shared by featured teacher Vennieta.

FEATURED TEACHER: Shifting the Climate

Vennieta

When I look at teachers who have put in the years—it is a really ugly place for a lot of us, you know. Some teachers are like, I am 10 years from retirement or I am coasting or I am just so broken down by this broken system, and so I embrace it and we should always reward anyone who has dedicated themselves to children and this profession because it's

(continued)

(continued)

very powerful. I guess that's what I kind of give the veteran title to—is like, time spent, but how you perceive yourself as a veteran has to be a lifelong learner.

Luckily, I have a little family of teachers that I've worked with for at least 16 years that have become a family. We also push each other a lot, coming to each other with things like "Hey, I have this opportunity for you to grow." It is a small group, but we're constantly pushing each other and being a support system for each other because we realize that we are veterans but we have a really huge responsibility that's beyond our students now, which is to mentor a group of teachers that come in.

Veteran teachers do create a climate for a school, and it's a huge responsibility. I wish more veteran teachers would acknowledge that. If you look at the job as piss poor, you can't stand it, you hate it, that trickles to your students but also trickles to the faculty. If you come in there with pride and you love your job and you love what we do—yes, there are some challenges that we have to address, but how are we going to address them? Let's think about this. Let's be solution oriented in this. I always liken it to being a surgeon or a doctor. I don't want my doctor to be a veteran and max out. When I go see the doctor, they need to have the freshest, newest idea for whatever is happening. Teaching is the same way. We have to constantly study our craft and refine our craft.

I'll tell you what, I'm trying to encourage more teachers to get on Instagram. If you're just a voyeur, you're just looking, but on any given day you have your ideas being challenged. Instagram drives me crazy, I need a break from it sometimes because of my inbox. Sometimes it's full of questions that people are asking, and I am like, "Why do you think I have time for that?" I was like, "Oh, man, this is another responsibility." But there are a lot of teachers that look at your Instagram because you're their veteran teacher because the veteran teachers may not want to embrace them.

Your interaction with someone can shift how someone sees the profession. Also, I remember my first huge meeting in our district. This veteran teacher came up to me, she had been teaching for 25 years at that point, and she walked up to me and gave me a prayer card. She said, "You have such a sweet, sweet spirit and I swear it resonates and I'm drawn to you." I thought, Oh, that's weird, and then she said, "I just want you to always protect the people that come after you because your heart's really pure in this." I still had that in my wallet.

With the cycle of admin coming in and out, sometimes the veteran teachers are more planted into a school community than the admin. We've had, I think, seven admins in nine years, seven principals. I'm one of those teachers who has been asked to be the principal before, you know, and pulled out of the classroom so many times, and it's just an utter respect for. . .I love what I do, and I feel like I can make the greatest impact in the classroom, but I also have an admin credential and I literally train teachers for a living. I think I can say things that maybe a new teacher can't say, so I will go and ask, "What's the problem? Okay, you stay here, I'm gonna go and say something, and then I'll take the ramifications for whatever it is." I think veteran teachers should use themselves in that way to where they position themselves to protect new teachers. I think that's important, and that's one of the reasons why I stay as a department chair.

Reflection Questions

1. What perceptions of "veteran teachers" do you hear coming through in Vennieta's statement? How do they compare to the perceptions you've held or heard about those who have stayed in the field for decades?
2. Veteran Teachers: Write a letter to yourself in your first years of teaching. What advice would you give yourself then to help you push through and hold onto themselves and their passion as they navigate the hills and valleys on the road ahead?
3. New or Incoming Teachers: Write a letter to yourself in your later years of teaching that you can read when the times get tough. What pieces of yourself do you want to remind yourself to hold onto? What encouragement can you give your future self to keep yourself grounded and connected with your purpose?

Conclusion

While there are certainly powerful lessons and benefits in communities that have veteran educators and staff, this chapter is certainly not a calling to stay at any costs. As covered in the chapter on the battles that often lead to teacher shortages, there is also much to be learned and gained from those who leave. Additionally, it is natural and expected that as one ages, their personal passions, interests and goals will shift and evolve—that they will come into themselves in new ways. The wisdom that the real Barbara Howards of the world give us is that often times when we are looking for the keys to unlocking better futures, the most powerful ones are woven into the identities of those who have stayed. In reality, what fuels teachers to stay is probably rooted in so many unique aspects of who they are as individuals that it might be impossible to create any sort of universal list or recipe that would speak to a large mass of individuals. However, the roots that ground veteran educators in their practice, their schools, and their communities often weave together generations of students, families, *and* educators.

REVISITING THE CRITICAL AUTOBIOGRAPHY: Reflecting on Veteran Teachers

Revisit the quote at the start of this chapter and reflect on who that person (or those people) are/were in the school's you've worked in and attended. What did they embody in their practice and being that stand out to you? What key lessons have they taught or modeled for you? How, if at all, do they show up in your teacher identity and practice?

References

Cohen, R. M. (2009). What it takes to stick it out: Two veteran inner-city teachers after 25 years. *Teachers and Teaching: Theory and Practice*, *15*(4), 471–491.

Day, C., & Gu, Q. (2009). Veteran teachers: Commitment, resilience and quality retention. *Teachers and Teaching: Theory and Practice*, *15*(4), 441–457.

National Center for Education Statistics. (2022). Teacher Turnover: Stayers, Movers, and Leavers. *Condition of Education*. U.S. Department of Education, Institute of Education Sciences. Retrieved [February 2022], from https://nces.ed.gov/programs/coe/indicator/slc

Chapter 5

Weaving Together the Mind and Body

They've taught you there are parts of you that you shouldn't love-that need to be smaller, quieter, bigger, louder, fixed, or changed. Love those pieces a little extra every day.

Instagram Post
@drcourtneyrose (July 10, 2021)

I am not going to lie. Sitting down to write this chapter was hard. In fact, this was the hardest chapter for me to write and it was not even an explicitly covered topic in the original proposal for this book. I talk about almost every aspect of my identity—race, gender, class. I have explored the nuanced experiences I have had around my hair texture, my skin complexion, and the way I speak. However, in all of that identity work, both public and private, I *never* talk about the one aspect of who I am that has presented some of the biggest and most consistent social and emotional challenges in my life—my weight and body size. To be clear, I think about this quite a bit. With all of the commercials, movies, television shows, social media ads, and so on focused on losing weight, it's almost impossible not to be consumed by these thoughts, especially when you're living in a body that has been deemed "fat," "too big," and "unfit." But unlike those other aspects of my identity, I never made connections between this aspect of my identity and life experience and my schooling/educational experiences, my decision to become an educator, *or* the ways in which I enact my pedagogical practices. In other words, I had never explored the development of my *physical identity* and its intersections with my academic, professional, or teacher identities.

This led me to think about the ways we discuss bodies, and particularly bodies that "do not fit" the dominant culture's expectations of what is healthy, desirable, professional, and right. More importantly, once I started weaving together my educational, schooling, and teaching experiences *through* my body, I found they were, and had always been, inextricably linked. Digging deeper, this oversight of the embodied experiences that students and educators have within schools points to the disconnect *from* the body that is often promoted through dominant social beliefs, instructional practices, and education policies. All of these revelations were sparked by an unexpected reaction during my morning routine.

At the start of 2023, I took on the common practice of paying more attention to my physical health through better workout and eating habits. About a month into my new routine, I was doing a dance workout. On the final section of the last song, I started crying—not an intense hysterical cry, but I felt a strong emotion coursing through my entire body and my eyes teared up, which oddly fueled me to push through the end of the workout. I literally had nothing left, but all of a sudden I just felt this surge of energy and emotion go through my body giving me just what I needed to complete the final moves. I finished the workout feeling so empowered, but as I turned off the workout, the emotion intensified and the tears just started flowing.

Reflecting on that moment, I recognize it as a necessary release, an opening of a valve triggered by the connection between my mental, emotional, and physical selves that I engaged in order to make it through to the end of the workout. I think the few years prior to restarting my health and fitness journey, with all of the shifts that the country went through, my transitioning into a new position and taking on more responsibilities and a heavier load as a full-time professor and different relationships in my life, changing, and evolving, I stored and held so much in my body, often mistreating and being very hard on it. But through all of that, my body never gave up on me. Sure, at times it gave me signals that I needed to do better or do differently. But it never stopped. It was there. It carried me and kept me whole. Digging deeper, I started to reflect on how as a Black person, as a Black woman, as a Black educator, I'd learned, and in some cases was explicitly taught, to store so much in my body, and that this is something I'd heard from so many other Black women, both inside and outside of education. We hold it, we carry it, we often use it to keep us going and occasionally we find different ways to release it. We find joyful ways, creative ways, powerful ways to release it, but often once we do, we're denigrated, chastised, and sometimes even killed.

This journey happens for our entire lives. These bodies that we were born into, can never just *be*, and as we figure out how to successfully and peacefully survive in the various spaces we occupy, we often learn to mistreat them, to chastise them, to hurt them. For many of us, these lessons are reinforced the strongest in schools as we carry our bodies through classrooms and buildings more often than not led by teachers and administrators whom we can't see ourselves in, and more importantly, who can't see themselves in us. Left unexplored, this chasm, or what the research refers to as a cultural gap or mismatch, often leads to the reproduction and reinforcement of deficit-based narratives, leaving many students trying to find safety and comfort in bodies that have been simultaneously labeled as "too much" and "not enough." Featured teachers, Joscelyn, Deonna, and Yari share some of the powerful revelations they came to as they viewed themselves and their practice through the eyes and experiences of their younger selves.

FEATURED TEACHERS: Re-membering Who I Am

Joscelyn

I had to learn how to trust myself and my story before I expected anything of my students. So once I made that sort of shift to be like, "Okay, talk to little Jocelyn." If I talked to her, she would not feel comfortable in the environment that you have laid out right now. If I myself would not feel comfortable sharing my likes, my dislikes, my connections to what we are learning, or how much I really want to know the person next to

(continued)

(continued)

me, how much I want to be their friend, or how much I want to know about the teacher in front of me or her life or whatever, then I am missing the mark. Once I thought about my classrooms through the lens of my little self, and reflected on what little Jocelyn would need to be comfortable in this space, I was focused on creating opportunities for students to grow into being comfortable. I was focused on community and being comfortable in community, and then once I was able to prioritize that, then I am like, "You guys, I am in the circle with you."

Deonna

Well, the first thing I carried with me was I never forgot about being that child, like that was such a warm-up formula to an influential place for me to be in because I will never forget what it's like to navigate that space and constantly have to code switch. That is not even the half of it. I went to a Montessori school and I really contributed my success to that school. But at the same time, they kind of "spirit-murdered" me, to use Bettina Love's language. They definitely snuffed out my being as a Black woman for sure because it had to be so tightly compartmentalized. It was a really interesting thing to reflect on it as an adult and to recognize what I gained and what I lost. I lost an ability to be rooted in my identity. My parents were great. They tried their best, they raised me, and I was raised outside of school in a Black community, but because that was my whole academic experience and that was what led me to be successful. I always knew that that person inside of me that was deeply rooted in Blackness and was excited to be Black had to assimilate pretty violently to something else. So, I always carried that with me.

Yari

The thing is, part of a formal training in teaching and part of the schooling training in teaching was to keep me from who I was. I knew who I was in an origin story that was told to me about me. Who I am now is the origin story I am claiming for myself, and so that is the active learning that happens every day because I feel like there is this spiritual manifestation that happens when you re-member yourself. For me, I don't know why this word is just coming up for me today, *serendipity*. Is that the God in me, the divine in me, the ancestors in me knew who I was. They pulled me, they guided me like, hey, Communications, Black Studies, English, like I did not know who I was then. But I was grappling. I was being guided. Who I am now is able to see that I was being carried, even though I didn't know [then]: This is who I am. I think now the more I learn of my history, and the real history that was kept from me. [I understand] that I was being sort of guided in a way that I didn't understand, but I understand that now. And the more that I know myself now, the more that I continue to uncover who I am and *whose* I am, shout out to Dr. Cynthia Dilliard. You know, I'm sort of tapping into becoming more of who she is, and I'm finding that power. But it comes with a lot of dissonance because I got to quiet the lies of my miseducation. Will Smith talks so powerfully in his book about this wall that he was building with his father, and I'm doing the opposite. You know, I'm not building a wall. I'm actually breaking down a wall to get to my truest self and it's like, that even makes me emotional because I have to grapple with rage. You know, I have to grapple with not feeling safe, I have to grapple with what love means for me, and so, it's, it's tough. When you're building it's full of hope and possibilities. When you are destroying, you know, it's full of smoke and clouds and you feel lost. But it's so crazy. You have to get there in order to get to. . .to get to the nothingness, but also the everything. Yeah, so I'm going through that process right now, and it's scary. It's beautiful. It's traumatic at times, but I am just remaining obedient and just open to just, not being the *best* version of myself but the *truest* version of myself that will allow me to be just such a different being to everybody else in my life.

Individual Reflection/Collective Discussion

1. Deonna speaks to the need to compartmentalize certain aspects of her identity throughout her educational journey. What pieces of

(continued)

(continued)

yourself were you encouraged to compartmentalize and/or separate from throughout your educational experiences? What messages did you internalize about these components of who you are and how you physically moved through and occupied space in schools and classrooms?

2. Joscelyn, Yari, and Deonna all reflect back on their younger selves and how realizing what they felt and needed as they moved through their schooling has impacted how they embody their current practice. If your younger self wrote you a letter, what do you think they would emphasize as they shared the physical experience of schooling? What messages did they internalize about who they are and could be and how do you see that manifesting in your own practice or vision for yourself as an educator?

As featured teachers Joscelyn, Deonna, and Yari share, facing and unlearning all of these lessons, liberating ourselves from these labels and relearning how to embrace, love, and care for our bodies is often the hardest piece of life's journey, but integral to stepping into the fullness of who we are and embodying practices that not only speak to the increasingly diverse students in our classrooms, but can also heal the pieces of us that our own K–12 journeys damaged. Speaking personally, this has certainly been one of the hardest parts of my life and one of the most instrumental and integral parts of what I bring to my work. In fact, it was in that moment described earlier in this chapter, as I sat on my couch crying after that workout that I realized that my relationship with my body and how I've felt as I moved through various spaces, particularly educational spaces, is why I feel it's so important to create learning environments in which students and teachers, especially Black students and teachers, can just *be*.

Many teacher education programs encourage or even require their pre-service teachers to explore the ways in which narratives of race, gender, class, and sexuality impact how their students view and are viewed within educational spaces. However, there is often very little opportunity for educators (either pre- or in-service) to unpack how they physically represent or embody these narratives. In her work "Thinking through the Flesh," Esther Ohito (2019) explores the ways that White educators often don't recognize how their presence shifts the racial dynamics within learning environments and the large selection of studies that focus on attending to the presence of whiteness in the teacher education space, White teacher candidates' discomfort and resistance to talking about issues of race, and the impacts on their identities as educators and how they embody and enact the curriculum.

Each semester, students in my own teacher education classes often gloss over the first question of the critical autobiography assignment that asks them to share their racial, ethnic, gender, sexual, and social class identities, and discuss any barriers and/or privileges associated with each. While many of the students of color dive right in and share in great depth and detail, many identifying as White or White Hispanic/Latiné find it a bit more challenging to fully express this component of their identity. Although they know the world sees or reads them as White, many communicate that they either don't think it's necessary to categorize themselves in that way or that they feel having to select that option doesn't fully capture how they see and are seen in the world.

This idea occasionally gets even more complicated for them when we dive into one of our early semester readings, Dyan Watson's "What Do You Mean When You Say 'Urban'?" As mentioned in Chapter 2, throughout my course, we engage in quite a bit of language analysis, critiquing how we use language to either disrupt or reproduce potentially damaging deficit-based narratives. Watson's reading powerfully explores how commonly used phrases like *urban* and *at risk* are used to mask racialized beliefs about BIPOC students and their communities. Finding interviews a powerful form of data through which to engage in this sort of discourse analysis, Watson interviewed predominantly White educators who were studying in a university-based teacher education program and unearthed many deficit-based narratives and beliefs about *urban* students, families, and communities. Upon digging deeper, Watson uncovered that many of these beliefs were not connected to the geographical location that these students inhabited, which is how many of *my* students define *urban* when asked to provide a definition, but rather the Black and Brown bodies through which they moved through the world. In this sense the educators' use of *urban* functioned as a code word or euphemism for race, making it impossible to dig into the racialized beliefs they held and the potential ways the teachers embodied them in their practice.

For example, in Watson's work, she found that many of the educators openly shared their beliefs about how urban students don't value education or want to learn as much as "other" students. When asked the definition of *urban* or to discuss urban teaching, the majority of teachers defined it as racially or ethnically diverse students and having to deal with the issues of race (Watson, 2011). This aligned with similar findings from previous studies, like Gilbert's 1997 study of 345 pre-service teachers in six universities. When reviewing this study, my White Hispanic/Latiné students often acknowledge that they've heard similar things said about themselves and their communities, but recognize that given the particular demographics of the area of South Florida in which many of them attended K–12 schooling, they may have had a drastically different experience of coming into their own racial/ethnic identity in different parts of the country, or even further north in the state. Additionally, many of the Black students in my courses are quick to point out that while the study focuses on the beliefs held and expressed by only White teachers, they've also heard these ideas shared by other Black teachers and non-White teachers of color. Again, as discussed in Chapter 2, if left unexplored, *any* educator of *any* racial/ethnic identity/background can enact and embody harmful narratives, reflecting deep internalization of them, including those about their own communities.

Disembodied Teaching/Teachers

There is a wide selection of research that points to the ways that traditional and dominant curriculum and pedagogical practices encourage and rely on a framing of the mind and body as separate from each other. So much of what lies at the root of dominant and traditional teaching practices is the control, policing, taming, and restraint of *the body* in an attempt to create more room for the mind to do its work. One of the core strategies that I remember learning in my own teacher education program was to teach students to engage in the active listening position, with both feet flat on the floor, hands clasped on their desks, and eyes tracking the speaker. It was assumed that if students were not fidgeting or playing with anything in their hands, then they were actively listening and engaged in the learning.

This separation of mind and body promotes the sort of detachment from *embodied* experiences that lead to critical self-awareness around racialized (and gendered, classed, and sexualized) experiences that many teachers of color, or those living at the intersections of marginalized identities, carry throughout their educational experiences and into their teaching practices. Returning to Ohito's (2019) work, she refers to this sort of teaching as a *disembodied pedagogy*, or one that "divorces the mind from the 'weeping, living, hurting body'" (p. 252). Just as in society at large, students of color are surveilled and policed at much higher rates. Predominantly White male school resource officers physically, and often violently, restrain Black students, many of whom are Black girls. As pointed out by Crenshaw, Ocen, and Nanda (2015) in Rose (2021): "First, Black boys are three times more likely to be suspended than White boys and Black girls are six times more likely to be suspended than are White girls." Furthermore Crenshaw et al. (2015) in Rose (2021) also point out that this disparity in disciplinary rates represents a critical problem and the initial piece in the school-to-prison pipeline. The American Civil Liberties Union (ACLU, n.d) explains this problem as follows:

> The pipeline begins with inadequate resources in public schools. Over crowded Classrooms, a lack of qualified teachers, and insufficient funding for "extras" such as Counselors, special education services, and even textbooks, lock students into Second-rate educational environments.

The data shows that when students are suspended from school, they are nearly three times more likely to be in contact with the juvenile justice system within the following year. Additionally, schools located in predominantly

Black and Brown communities often have more strict policies for how students are able to express themselves through dress with the enforcement of uniforms and attempt to learn under a strong police presence from the moment they walk into the school building as they pass through metal detectors and have their bodies and belongings searched, often internalizing messages that their bodies have more potential to hold and enact violence than the bodies of their White and more affluent counterparts.

Reflecting on this, I agree that, yes, many of us currently teaching were asked to, in many ways, separate mind from body (and spirit) during our own journeys through public education as increased emphasis on standardized testing and accountability pushed for and rewarded a "sameness," not only in action but thought within the educational process. However, when engaging teachers in processes of critical self-reflection, and through my own journey back into myself, it is clear that the further our body is from the widely accepted and desired norm, the less we are ever truly able to disconnect from our bodies. We simply learn to suppress or reframe these painful experiences in order to make it through and survive. Looking back to Deonna's comments, we can see her still contributing her success to the institution that, in her own words, "spirit-murdered" her through the lack of explicit discussion and acknowledgment of how race was playing into her embodied learning experiences.

Disembodied teaching encourages a distancing from the physical and emotional signals our bodies are giving us, viewing them as potential hindrances and barriers to the learning process. I have worked with so many educators who shy away from engaging students in explorations of real-world issues and topics because they are afraid of the emotions they might bring up and losing control of the lesson and the students. We've been taught that learning is a neat process that occasionally requires hard work, but more or less happens devoid of feeling. It is a cognitive process that can be mastered through the memorization and mimicking of concrete strategies. Teachers learn the strategies in teacher education programs and professional development sessions and then pass them on to students, mildly dressing them up to make them age appropriate and engaging. But learning, by nature, is an act of leaning into discomfort, facing the tensions that arise as we engage in dialogue that makes us squirm, viewing the ills of the world not as phenomena that is experienced by other bodies but exploring why they are not experienced by our own, and facing the feelings that come with that. Disembodied teaching dehumanizes both student and educator, requiring both to act now and feel later. Featured teacher Ryan shared some reflections on his process of leaning into the discomfort of opening up difficult conversations within his practice.

FEATURED TEACHER: Courageous Conversations Compass

Ryan

I do a lot of work engaging adults in courageous conversations centering race, and there's this protocol for it. I don't know if you heard of them, like Glenn Singleton, but he's the creator. I'm not shopping for him, but you know, I do believe in his work and I tried to apply it in the work that I do. But what we are speaking to is like these four agreements that are really centered on staying engaged, speaking your truth, experiencing discomfort, and then accepting and expecting non-closure, which is hard for folks. Then, we will also get to the second part of the protocol. It is this compass and you use the compass as a way to center yourself in difficult conversations, especially about race. But there is the feeling quadrant, there's the thinking quadrant, an acting quadrant, and a moral quadrant. The tendency, especially for White folks, those practicing whiteness, even in the realm of assimilation, is to come with the thinking and wanting to think and quickly do as opposed to processing and feeling as a way to inform the doing. It's not like we use the compass to catch people to be like, "Oh, you're in that quadrant and you're wrong." It is not that at all. But the idea is to kind of get to understand where you are, know that you have the ability to actually move around that compass and then to check where other people are entering so that you can see who has a capacity to be able to have this conversation.

(continued)

(continued)

Individual Reflection/Collective Discussion

1. Ryan's comments emphasize the role between emotions and critical reflection/dialogue. Looking back on your own K–12 experiences, were you encouraged to sit in the emotions that arose during the learning process? If so, what approaches and strategies did your educators use to help you manage and process those emotions? If not, what do you WISH they would have done?
2. Whether your answer to question 1 is yes or no, how did the relationship that was fostered between emotions and learning impact the development of your academic identity and your physical comfort in schools and classrooms?

Loving and Caring for Your Body as Resistance and Liberation

During the shift to virtual teaching that much of the country, and world, experienced between spring 2020 and summer 2021, I found myself teaching sitting down for the majority of the time, staring into a computer screen teaching up to 40 other boxes—most with nothing but a black screen and name written in white print. Upon the end of the spring 2021 semester, I posted a thread of images to my Instagram page outlining the lessons learned from that academic year. Number one on the list was that teaching is a whole body experience. In my typical instruction style I am known to wander around the room and take up as much space as possible, a far cry from the girl who literally did her best to shrink and hide herself during the latter portions of her K–12 experiences. As an educator, everything from my hair to my fingernails are a part of my instruction. When we shifted to virtual learning, I initially felt lost and unsure of how to provide the same level of engagement and connection with both the academic content, and between myself and my students.

Early in the process of writing this book, I had the pleasure of hearing Dr. Jamila Lyiscott, scholar and author of *Black Appetite, White Food: Issues of Race, Voice, and Justice Within and Beyond the Classroom*, speak as the keynote at my university's annual social justice summit. During the speech, she presented her framework for a Liberated Literacy Pedagogy, which at one point led her to speak about her personal battle with her weight. She spoke of how she realized that if her work on loving and caring for Black students and Black people didn't extend to, or begin with loving and caring for her own Black body, then it was out of alignment. This encouraged her to take more care with how she treated herself and her body, what she put in it, how she moved it, how she thought and spoke about it to create that alignment. The conscious commitment and practice to love her own Black body strengthened and fueled her work even further. Sitting there in the audience that day, I realized that just like she shared, my battle with my weight or feelings about my weight was a symbolic representation of the internalized narratives about the value of my own Black body. For most of my life, the internal dialogue when starting a new exercise or eating regimen was always one of creating a body that would make others feel more comfortable. In other words, I was eating better and working out because I hated my body, and I hated it because of the feelings others had about it, or my perceptions of those feelings.

In that moment, I consciously reframed my thinking from working out and eating healthier because I hate my body to doing so because I love my body. Rooting myself in this new space of radical self-love doesn't always make the workouts more enjoyable, keep me from the roller coaster that is feeling comfortable in one's own skin, or immediately bring the occasional negative self-talk to a stop. Healing journeys just don't work that way. However, similar to Dr. Lyiscott's revelations, it has helped me to feel more rooted in, connected to, and aligned with the commitments I have to the development of liberating environments and experiences (both inside and outside of schools and classrooms) as I embody this practice for *myself*. It has opened up deeper understandings of my own K–12 experiences as I look at them from a perspective that I'd spent the majority of my life avoiding or trying to distance myself from, which only limited my capacity to humanize myself and my work. Featured teacher Bobby provides an example of how embodying our commitments as teachers can actually be an instructional tool in and of itself.

FEATURED TEACHER: Embodied in Me

Bobby

So I'm out loud in front of them. I'm wearing shirts that talk about Black joy, and Black excellence. I want them to ask questions about how I walk, what I wear, what I do. They say "You always wear these shirts Mr. Morgan." "Yes, I do. Yes, I do. Why? Well, you liked these things, right?" "Yes, but why else? Why else would I do this? You want us to see them?" "Yes. That's why. Why do I want you to see this?" Get, you know, they give you like the "I don't know." Right? But by the end of the conversation, I have buy-in from young people who know that regardless of how far or how little they have come in my class, that I need them to know that their dignity, their joy, their strength, their resilience, the respect that they command, all of that stuff is going to be embodied in me. And it's going to be embodied in how I treat them.

Individual Reflection/Collective Dialogue

Bobby describes the way he shows up and embodies his teaching as "out loud." What do you think he means by this? What would it look like for you to show up "out loud" in front of your students?

Conclusion

As educators, if we truly want to develop spaces in which our students feel affirmed, valued, accepted, and loved, we have to recognize that this work starts with showing and embodying those feelings for and about ourselves *first*. We have to recognize that the ways that we allow our bodies to be talked about and treated is often a manifestation of the internalized narratives that we have learned throughout our own childhoods, both inside and outside of schools. As pointed out by Tricia Hersey in her book *Rest Is Resistance: A Manifesto*:

> We proudly proclaim showing up to work or an event despite an injury, sickness, or mental break. We are praised and rewarded

> for ignoring our body's need for rest, care and repair. The cycle of grinding like a machine continues and becomes internalized as the only way. (Hersey, 2022)

A great place for educators to start the work of creating and embodying liberating learning environments is to unpack these narratives, identify the pieces of who you are that you were taught needed to be fixed, changed, hidden, was not professional, or intelligent enough, was too big or too loud, was too distracting or not interesting enough. Then, love and care for those pieces of yourself unapologetically and fiercely. As you do, note any revelations that come up for you, explore how those internalized narratives were rooted in racist, classist, sexist, and other damaging ideologies, and how the way you physically showed up and took up space may have reproduced and reinforced these narratives and ideologies, both implicitly/unintentionally and explicitly/intentionally.

REVISITING THE CRITICAL EDUCATIONAL AUTOBIOGRAPHY: Embodied Teaching

Return to your Critical Educational Autobiography and reflect on the following questions, and add the new information to the appropriate sections:

1. Reflecting on the quote at the start of this chapter, what pieces of yourself were you taught needed to be smaller, louder, bigger, fixed, or changed? In what ways were these messages (re)produced or reinforced throughout your schooling experienced?
2. How, if at all, have you embodied these messages in your teaching OR disrupted them *through* the embodiment of your teaching?

References

American Civil Liberties Union (ACLU) (n.d.). School-to-prison pipeline. Retrieved from https://www.aclu.org/racial-justice/what-school-prison-pipeline

Gilbert, S. L. (1997). The "four commonplaces of teaching": Prospective teachers' beliefs about teaching in urban schools. *The Urban Review*, *29*(2), 81–96.

Hersey, T. (2022). *Rest Is Resistance: A Manifesto*. Hachette, UK.

Lyiscott, J. (2019). *Black Appetite, White Food: Issues of Race, Voice, and Justice Within and Beyond the Classroom*. Routledge.

Ohito, E. O. (2019). Thinking through the Flesh: A critical autoethnography of racial body politics in urban teacher education. *Race Ethnicity and Education*, *22*(2), 250–268

Rose, P. R. (2021). *Health Equity, Diversity, and Inclusion: Context, Controversies, and Solutions*. Jones & Bartlett Learning.

Watson, D. (2011). What do you mean when you say "urban." *Rethinking Schools*, *26*(1), 48–50.

Chapter 6

Weaving Together Theory and Practice by Weaving Yourself into Your Practice

Teaching and leading vulnerably pushes back against narratives that force people to "prove" or "earn" their value and humanity as you lead with your own.

Twitter and Instagram Post
@drcourtneyrose (October 10, 2022)

While studying for my Masters at the Harvard Graduate School of Education (HGSE, or affectionately referred to as HUG-SEE by students/faculty), I had one remaining elective course requirement to fill and decided to use this opportunity to venture onto the main campus, enrolling in a course on international hip-hop identities. Personal struggles in identity development attracted me to anything involving explicit exploration of the topic, and I figured it would, at the very least, be a fun and interesting note on which to close out my time as a Harvard graduate student. The class was held in Harvard's newly opened Hiphop Archive & Research Institute. The walls were covered with images of African American musicians, actors, and their work (movie posters, album art, etc.). The space in which the actual instruction was performed was almost the complete antithesis of the antiquated, White-washed spaces I had come to expect from higher learning institutions, particularly Harvard, and served as a physical representation of the hip-hop elements and culture.

The foundation of the course was deep, personal engagement with the hip-hop element *knowledge of self*. We developed two hip-hop names and personas. One was used for "stage performance" (classroom participation) during all class sessions. The other was used for our writing, the majority of which was in a journal where we explored the ways our identities shaped and were shaped by our experiences and interpretations of messages in media, music, and society at large. These personas did not need to be similar to each other in terms of communication style, but we were encouraged to make sure that we were always *representin'* (Irizarry, 2009) one or more of the identities that comprised our actual selves. This was my first, albeit surface-level, introduction to the concept of intersectionality, the understanding that "who we are" is composed of multiple selves all of which shape and are shaped by our interactions with others and hold varying degrees of value in different spaces and contexts.

Although school was always a space in which I experienced academic success, never before had I been so connected to academic content. On a daily basis we were asked to "come as who we were" and to truly think about how constructions of our identities (both our own and those others/society imposed upon us) were simultaneously shaped by and shaping our experiences, beliefs, and actions. Together, we explored the ills of society, breaking down explicit and implicit messages of privilege, access, oppression, and constructions of race, gender, and sexuality, always taking time to reflect on how we were positioned within them, much as we've done throughout the course of this text. It was a communal study of individual and collective identities where each person felt supported in the discomfort of exploring the ways in which "who we were" in various spaces disrupted, and in some cases, reproduced the conditions for inequities to persist.

Engaging in this level of critical analysis helped me find a new voice accompanied with a surprising sense of freedom and hope. I began to acknowledge the ways I played a role in my own *oppression* through the conscious and unconscious *suppression* of various parts of my identity in an effort to "fit in" and adjust to my surroundings. Through this process of continued reflection and analysis I could easily see that I had within me the power to *take action* toward change, if only I'd allow myself to move, and most importantly, *teach* through the fullness of my authentic identity.

Theory-Practice Gap

A large subset of teacher education research aims to address the tendency for educators who leave courses and programs rooted in critical, innovative, culturally responsive, equity-driven, and social justice–oriented pedagogical theories and approaches unsure of how to put them into practice within their specific teaching contexts. Known as the *theory-practice gap*, this phenomenon is often rooted in a lack of firsthand experience and *active* engagements with these theories and approaches or the realities facing many public school students and educators *prior* to stepping into the classroom. While many teacher education programs are producing courses with syllabi stacked with texts and activities that create opportunities for pre- and in-service teachers to reflect on the *what* and *why* of these theories and approaches, the dominant instructional practices and models for other components of the programs (i.e., classroom observations and student teaching) remain rooted in traditional approaches that give little insight into the *how*. Coupled with teacher evaluation practices, reported lack of structural and administrative support, many teachers find themselves abandoning the critical, humanizing, student-driven theories and approaches that fueled their passions during their teacher education programs or enacting surface-level versions of them that do little to transform educational environments and experiences. Unfortunately, I can speak to this personally.

During my first year of teaching fifth grade, armed with the language of culturally responsive education, I spent the summer developing a classroom vision around the goals of *high academic achievement* and the development of a *critical consciousness* that would foster a sense of urgency and a path to action leading my students to disrupt the status quo (Ladson-Billings, 1999; Gay, 2018). Noting my students' interest in and identification with rap music and hip-hop culture, and remembering the transformative experience from the course I'd taken at Harvard, I attempted to recreate that space for my students. As a math/science teacher, I struggled to find ways to integrate some of the practices of my professor, unsure of where the work needed to start with my fifth graders. I finally settled on beginning with the use of rap as a hook to engage my students, incorporating materials from canned programs that used rap to teach students various skills such as multiplication and division tables. While initially this worked as a means to draw them in, it did very little to keep them engaged. I quickly began to feel the pressure of meeting demands amid time constraints, mandates on the use of scripted curriculum, and random administrative observations within the increasingly test-based competition-driven culture of my school (and the culture of public schooling at large). Feeling exhausted and unsupported, I abandoned my vision and did my best to fall in line with school, district, and state-wide requirements.

As mentioned in the Introduction, I find it difficult to reflect on my first year of teaching as it forces me to come face-to-face with the ways in which I feel like I did not show up for myself or my students. It would be easy to place the blame solely on the culture of schooling in which conforming to standardized practices designed around the social norms of society come in direct conflict with many educators' attempts at creating spaces that require and value authentic culturally specific ways of knowing and expressing knowledge. Unquestionably, these structural issues play a major part in teachers' perceptions of their abilities to effectively engage in critical culturally responsive practices, and I think it is important for educators and society to acknowledge and name these constraints and barriers. However, I approach this work with the stance that as "teacher" I played a central role in reinforcing and validating the barriers to enacting such practices within the context of my classroom. Therefore, examining the shortcomings of my attempts to transform teaching and learning with and for my students always begins with the exploration of how to bring who I was/am into my practice, which will open up more opportunities and more clear pathways to becoming the teacher my students need, and ultimately, bridging both the theory-practice and self-practice gaps that often create distance between ourselves and our students.

Fueled by these reflections on my own teaching experiences and the memory of the powerful space that I'd experienced during that Harvard course, the focus for my doctoral studies was rooted in preparing educators to comprehensively enact practices rooted in the expression of authentic identities (both their students and their own). I landed on a study specifically exploring the development, implementation, and interpretation of a university-based course that prepared teachers to enact pedagogy rooted in the hip-hop cultural ways of knowing and being, again deeply connecting with its emphasis on the need to have and incorporate a strong knowledge of *self*. The study's findings supported existing research presenting university-based teacher education as a "value-added" endeavor (Darling-Hammond, 2006). For many of the enrolled pre- and in-service teachers, the most powerful component of the course was the fact that it was held within the walls of a university and served as one of the few spaces in which they could *experience* the type of critical, culturally relevant, and social justice–oriented pedagogy they read about in their other courses and which was prevalent within the language of the mission statements that drew them to the university and their selected programs. In this regard, the course answers the call for transformational student-driven learning experiences to address the unmet needs and desired learning experiences as expressed *by teachers* entering/working in culturally, socially, and linguistically diverse classrooms.

Further, analysis of the study's findings drew attention to continued tensions at the intersection of policy, practice, and power impacting dominant narratives about effective and valuable approaches to both teacher education *and* teaching within K–12 environments. If the aim of university-based courses and programs is to prepare effective educators for the cultural diversity of today's public school classrooms, there must be a re-imagining, or remixing, of what effective professional preparation and practice for teachers is within these racially, culturally, and linguistically diverse contexts (Darling-Hammond, 2010). Specifically, within the politically-charged climate of the teacher education landscape, transformative teacher educators and curriculum/course developers must conceptualize their roles as activists and advocates, combining "moral convictions and courage, critical analyses, and political activism with high-quality curriculum and instruction" (Gay, 2005, p. 224).

This research spoke to the need for teacher education for the *enactment* of culturally relevant social justice and equity-oriented pedagogy to disrupt and act in opposition to the "overwhelming presence of Whiteness" within university-based programs (Ladson-Billings, 2005; Sleeter, 2000). Even with the employment of recruitment and retention efforts aiming to increase racial and cultural diversity among university-based teacher education faculty and student bodies, pre-service teacher education remains stuck in narratives of meritocracy and White supremacy. More specifically, contentious political debates often arise concerning where to place courses rooted in diverse ways of knowing and being within university-based programs of study as well as who should/can teach them and how they should be taught. As a result, these courses are often watered down to make them more palatable for the predominantly White student body, relegated to the margins of the program of study as electives or optional courses and/or the topics are woven into other courses limiting the depth in which they can be explored and reflected upon by pre- and in-service teachers (Gay, 2005; Ladson-Billings, 2005).

My study provided a snapshot of one enactment of this type of teacher education course in a university-based teacher education program, and was driven by my belief that new directions are needed to revitalize teaching and learning for today's increasingly diverse youth population. Noting the growing body of research highlighting approaches rooted in diverse cultural frames of reference that serve as the dominant languages and lenses of today's youth, it seemed like a potentially fruitful, yet unexplored, area through which to transform dominant approaches within teacher education. Additionally, given the role that institutions of higher learning play in perpetuating practices and narratives that contribute to the continued marginalization of certain populations, I found it critical to explore the enactment of an approach aimed at the disruption of such practices and narratives from *within*.

Throughout my time in the course, I was struck by the amount of passion that was evoked from the depth and energy of the conversations each week. Guided by hip-hop's emphasis on critical self-analysis and authenticity, and the professor's own commitment to transforming narratives impacting the educational experiences of traditionally marginalized populations, he pushed the enrolled teachers to dig into the nuances of hip-hop culture to unearth new pedagogical tools and critical understandings of their socio-political positions in society (Emdin, 2011). As a result, the course often challenged the enrolled teachers, bringing them face-to-face with uncomfortable revelations about their own privileges and biases and the impact these have on the ways in which they view and engage with their students.

For example, one enrolled pre-service teacher, who identified as a White woman, reflected on the revelations that arose from the discomfort and awkwardness she felt while engaging in some of the course activities that pushed students to embody hip-hop culture's practice of expression rhythm and creative processes. Specifically, she reflected on the weekly opening cypher, in which the entire class stood in a circle and the professor or a volunteer would create the initial beat on which the remaining students would build by adding their own vocals or percussive beats. This was usually done by banging on the table (with hands, fists, or other items like water bottles or books), beat boxing (creating percussive sounds using the lips, tongue and vocal chords), or hand claps and feet stomping. Going around the circle in a predetermined direction, each student would weave and layer in their contribution creating a collaborative and dynamic piece. In her reflection, this student noted that the weekly participation in this activity made her recognize the way that her schooling, up until that point, had been geared toward *her* strengths as a White student and that this course opened up to a much larger group of people to show *their* strengths.

By experiencing the discomfort of having to adapt to a learning environment rooted in the norms of a different culture, this student experienced firsthand what many Black and Latiné students experience when entering schools operating from the norms of dominant (read White, middle/upper class) members of society. All of the participants in my study, except for one, had K–12 schooling in the United States, the majority of which were public schools. The immersive experience of the course challenged *all* of their preconceptions of how learning environments should look and sound, regardless of their own racial/ethnic, gender, and cultural identities, particularly within the walls of their prestigious university. For some, like the student mentioned, their experience in the course exposed the ways that they had not only become complicit in the continued oppression and marginalization of urban, predominantly Black and Latiné youth, but also themselves as educators, as their own experiences in the K–12 system taught them to disengage their emotions from the teaching and learning process. Analysis of interview and observation data revealed how the opportunity to emotionally engage with material fostered a deep, long-lasting connection with both the course and the professor.

While the course, much like the one I took at Harvard, was strongly influenced by the practices and artifacts of hip-hop culture, to both the professor and the enrolled teachers it was much bigger than hip-hop. The immersive experience of the course awakened new sensibilities and revitalized the teachers' passions and commitments to enacting critical and culturally relevant practices aimed at equity and social justice. Thus, based on my findings I suggested, and still suggest, university-based teacher education programs and educators seeking to adequately equip teachers with the necessary tools with which to enact transformational pedagogical practices need to provide them with equally transformational experiences *within* their teacher education courses. Doing so will provide the enrolled pre- and in-service teachers with new cultural frames of reference, welcoming new perspectives rooted in the realities of their future students and opening new possibilities for the disruption of the status quo.

Teaching Vulnerably

My first official job as a professor was working as an adjunct, or part-time, professor for a university-based teacher academy. The program was in its first year, and I joined in the spring semester teaching one section of a course on educational assessment. As a part of the program, the students evaluate their professors twice, once at the mid-semester point and once at the end of the semester. Around the time of the mid-semester evaluations, I received an email from the program's director saying he wanted to meet with me about the results. Admittedly, I was a bit nervous because the results had not been directly released to us and I had no idea what it said. In fact, to this day I still have not seen them. During our meeting, he told me my evaluations were incredible and asked me what I was doing to get those results. More specifically, based on the comments students left, he was curious about what I thought they were connecting with so deeply. I remember being a little taken aback by the question and taking a minute to think about what he was asking and whether the answer could even be put into words. Honestly, I don't remember *exactly* what my response was, but I do know that stepping into the teacher educator role I wanted to challenge what my students thought about how teaching could and should look and feel.

As is typical for an adjunct, at the start of that first semester I was teaching from a syllabus that I had absolutely no part in creating. From the selection of readings to the order of topics, and even the assignments and assessments, everything was already planned and my role was to deliver the content. Now, obviously as an adjunct, you are encouraged to add your own touch and deliver the content as you see fit, but for some reason in the first couple of weeks of facilitating the class, I felt it incredibly challenging to find a flow and rhythm. Eventually, I realized that I'd fallen into a similar practice as early on in my K–12 teaching years. I was enacting a *performance* of "professor" that was rooted in the practices and models of professors whose classes had a profound impact on me, but did not have enough of *me* in it.

While I felt that my students were walking away with clear understandings of the content and the space overall felt enjoyable, most days I left feeling like there was a bit of a disconnection between the students and the content that was rooted in the disconnection they could likely feel between me and the content, and as a result, between me and them. In other words, I was bringing a version of Dr. Rose into the space that in many ways left necessary pieces of Courtney outside, making it impossible to facilitate the development of a truly humanizing and collaborative learning environment. Although I felt like I was emulating the practices of professors who had challenged pre-existing notions of what a professor could and should be, in leaving pieces of my own authentic self out of the room and out of my practice, I was unintentionally reproducing a culture rooted in the narrative that in learning experiences/communities it's better to come as who you *think you should be*, who others *expect you to be*, rather than *who you are*.

Sharing myself in this way felt risky, but I remembered the *feeling* of sitting in the course in Harvard, exploring the course of focus in my doctoral research and engaging in the spaces and experiences created by others who had transformed what I thought was possible for and through the art of teaching. So I began where I felt comfortable, sharing stories of my life, much like I've done throughout this book. I shared stories of my time as a student, as a teacher, as a daughter, as a romantic partner, as a woman, as a *Black* woman. I shared them when they felt appropriate or necessary to support the climate and culture I was attempting to cultivate with my students. I'm sure these stories worked to humanize me, to weave together my professional and personal identities and enable me to teach as both "Courtney" and "Dr. Rose." However, over time, these continued (and sometimes terrifying) acts of sharing pieces of myself and my story also began to open opportunities for my students to share theirs, turning our personal journeys through schooling and education into additional texts for the course and humanizing the content, creating deep ties to "the work."

Developing a model for a pedagogy of vulnerability, multicultural and peace educator, Brantmeier (2013) speaks directly to the humanizing power of leading with vulnerability and identity into their instructional practice, stating:

> If the educator opens [their] identity and life up for examination as part of the lived curriculum of the classroom, students will model that self-examination and go deeper in their learning; learning becomes relevant, has value beyond the classroom, and new meaning is constructed in the process. (p. 3)

These sentiments are also shared by our featured teachers Ryan and Vennietta, who share the role that bringing the fullness of themselves into their practice and leading with vulnerability played in opening new pathways to knowing and seeing their students:

FEATURED TEACHERS: Teaching Vulnerably

Ryan

My experience has been connecting at the human level, through a sincere conversation of wanting to really know the people that are in front of me, and sharing myself in that process, and not just the beautiful pieces but the ugly ones as well. I didn't even have language for them. I guess they call it a check-in now or circling up. It's almost like how we ignited this conversation today. You didn't jump in and be like, alright, "The first question that I have for you is." There was a conversation. I don't know how to name it all, but it was checking in on the human level.

There are different things I like when I am coaching educators. I can name some specific things. I can name the value of names and give strategies to actually become very much in touch with them. Like, write that student's name over and over again. Write their name on a folder, make it pop, see the value in their name and what that does for the relationship between you and that student. Or another strategy is to open up spaces and pathways for [your students] to actually be able to connect with you on a human level. So that could be through conversation, right?

We did note exchanges with students, we did sticky note passes. There are different things that I could package, but at the heart of it, at the very root of it is feeling naturally and sincerely that there is a value in the people in front of you to begin with. Because, honestly, all these educators out here, you got access to strategies at your fingertips. Right now, we could probably come up with 1,000. Just Google it. That isn't it. We are the strategy, and that has everything to do with us doing an archeological dig of self in a way that is vulnerable, in a way that is critical of self and loving at the same time.

I have been socialized to actually think and believe certain things and my values are based on those beliefs, and those beliefs and values inform what it is that I do and how I show up and how I engage interpersonally. So I very much feel like yes [bring yourself into the space].

(continued)

(continued)

It's like, how do you *not* do that? There are strategies that we can name that will show people how and I have seen them. So, ways in which we can set folks up who might not know, like, because I am not in a position to shame. People are where they are. But for me to say, how was it that I brought Ryan into the space? I don't know how [I] cannot, and I don't know how you can*not* put the spirits and the lived experiences and the cultures of the students first, as a platform to build the teaching and learning experience.

If you are familiar with Harry Wong, who wrote about the first two weeks of school. It gives you routines and procedures. Some of it is dope, but it's the first two weeks of school. Dr. Wong, you know what I mean? It's like, that joint gotta be consistent all the time because we are ever evolving. And so I think that it has a lot to do with self-awareness and bringing consciousness to the personal work-archeological dig. That's how that enables me to bring myself constantly, as Ryan Parker, in the space.

Vennieta

There are so many little things that we do that impact students. So with that knowledge of all these stories that I've heard from students, I want to create this environment that [makes them feel] so safe with the little things that I do there. Whether it's the act of kindness, whether it's transfer of knowledge, whether it's building competence in the classroom—if I'm asking all these high expectations of my students, they got to know who they're talking to, they got to know when they walk in my door, that I will defend them, that I protect them, that it's a safe place for them to be themselves.

A lot of that is me telling them about me, you know, my classroom has to feel like *our* home, they have to know about me, my life too. They have to know that I'm vulnerable to them and that I want the best for them that my intentions are pure for them. I talk about the realities of the world, the realities of the classroom, the reality of our community, there's really nothing that's off-limits in my classroom.

Another large part of it is creating a curriculum for students that's challenging for them. They have to know they're smart, they have to know that I believe in them every single day. When I'm disappointed in them, they know it, so we talk about it. And so it's like, it's like [the learning environment] has to be safe. It has to be a place of honesty, and I can't ignore all the things that are happening outside. But when they walk in my classroom, that has to be a safe place. So it's this kind of just mindfulness of how things that I do impact [my students] every single day.

Individual Reflection/Collective Discussion:

1. At one point in Ryan's comments, he states, "We are the strategy." How do you interpret this statement and how does that shed light on what it means to teach and lead vulnerably?
2. Vennietta speaks of her classroom as being a "safe space." How can teaching and leading vulnerably help to ensure that the classroom is a safe space for a diverse group of students who may all have different beliefs and needs within the learning environment?

Creating a Culture of Trust

One of the key outcomes of integrating who you are into your practice and leading with humanity and vulnerability is that it can help to cultivate learning communities rooted in *trust*. As previously covered, at the time of writing this book, states are continuing to pass bill after bill attempting to place stronger parameters on what teachers can and cannot teach. This large push for greater curricular and pedagogical control may feel new to some, but has roots in a long-standing distrust between various stakeholders in the education process. Narratives of "persistent achievement problems" and "deficient teaching" fueled by federally funded reports like the National Commission on Excellence in Education's (1983) *A Nation at Risk* painted pictures of a failing public school system that was leaving American students falling behind in global performance measures. In the wake of such reports, politicians and policymakers pushed market-based strategies like standardized curricula, standardized testing, and licensure requirements designed to hold schools and teachers accountable and promote more "effective teaching." However, these efforts often reduced teaching and learning to rote technical and mechanical skills (Adams & Forsyth, 2009). These efforts further deprofessionalized the work of teachers, fueling narratives that *anyone* who can read the curriculum can teach the curriculum and set the stage for what would later evolve into the mass exodus from the classroom many districts experienced in the 2021–2022 and 2022–2023 school years.

Additionally, with testing policies and practices often ignoring the many social, cultural, and political factors that impact processes of teaching and learning, the results of tests were often used to justify deficit-based narratives that placed the problems in the individuals (i.e., students, parents, educators) rather than the structures and systems in which the people operated. Specifically, the high-stakes nature of the standardized testing and accountability movements exacerbated pre-existing inequities as tests served as gatekeepers to accessing various funds, resources, and opportunities that disproportionately impacted schools serving Black, Brown, and other historically disenfranchised populations. Failure to acknowledge the historical and intensifying social and cultural issues of an increasingly diversifying population and a schooling system that prioritizes standardization and uniformity resulted in ideological battles and power struggles that, in many cases, intensified the distrust between schools and communities, teachers and administrators, teachers and parents, and teachers and students. As such, many identify the development of stronger social or relational trust as the foundational step in the reforming and transformation of educational environments and communities (Bryk & Schneider, 2002; Ladson-Billings, 2005). To that end, creating spaces rooted in vulnerable sharing can help teachers, students, and parents/families/caretakers identify points of connection that can unravel false narratives and shift the culture and climate of the learning environment. Featured teachers Alexia and Joscelyn share their experiences in teaching through vulnerability as a practice and *process* of earning and re-earning trust from the communities of learners and parents/families they serve.

FEATURED TEACHER: Trust as Process

I would say trust is probably the most important thing, especially when you are dealing with different cultures, different trauma, different people in general. You know, we do not just put our trust into people we do not know. We do not put trust into people that do not take time. I believe trust comes with value. So if you value someone, then you know you are building their trust. Like, okay, I will smile in your face. But I know what you are about.

So, I think, as educators and our students, do we trust the system? Absolutely not. Do we trust all of our leaders? I think that is a big, big problem for the adults, but also for the kids. And I think, all around, building that trust includes getting to know someone, and again, that is the human aspect of it. So if you are just a paper pusher, and you are just trying to get this done to sign this document and say, Okay, well, we just got this grade, it becomes a factory and not a place where learning and growing can happen. You are just trying to meet this imaginary target that is not even true. Because all of those things are based on money and corporations anyway.

So I think that trickles down to the parents. So if you cannot build trust, then we cannot really be genuine with our love. We cannot have anything without trust and joy and love in these situations, especially when we are talking about people and not things. So I would really hope that people just take the time to slow down a little bit. When we can trust, we can hear what people are saying, and we can value and really listen and not just be like, alright, they want that. Whatever, we are going to keep doing our thing over here.

I think we are losing feelings and just doing things because we have to do them and not doing things because there is a love there for them. With my kids, I want to make sure that they trust me and I say it every day. Well, it's Mrs. P's job to keep you safe, to keep you loved, to keep you happy and learning, and they know. Like we said in our morning

(continued)

(continued)

meeting, is this a safe place? If it is not a safe place am I doing my job? I'm not. Yeah, and I want them to know that. Because when you are safe, you feel vulnerable, you feel protected, you feel loved, and you feel valued. I want to see that happening in my classroom first because I know it is a possibility, and I think if we can see that it's real, and it can happen, then hopefully, it will trickle down to other areas and things. But I think it's important that we have these conversations and that educators get together and discuss these things. And then we inform the parents and then we start changing how this thing is.

Joscelyn

And so like, trust, I learned about what is true about stress, and how we're wired through stress, the impact of a relationship being planted, a trusting relationship being planted, and how that changes our stress dynamics from toxic to tolerable when we have those trusting adults that are able to buffer and mitigate the impact of stress and trauma on the growing brain and body. Like, it's a no brainer. It's like, okay, so if I create calm, safe, predictable environments, in classrooms, that in and of itself, in my presence, as a trusting adult, mitigates stress and trauma from the outside world. When students come through the threshold of my classroom, I am actually rewiring, reworking that biological mechanism of stress in their brains and bodies. It blows my mind, and just me doing that is actually changing their bodies, not just their environments, not just their experience, but inside their bodies.

We know about a lot of the you know, the body effects of what stress can do and how it can break down our immune systems and everything. I remember my kids used to be out a lot with stomach issues, asthma, all this and I used to be like, why? When I gained a deeper understanding of the impacts of stress on the body, I'm like, no wonder because I knew what they were going through outside of my classroom. It's no wonder that those experiences were manifesting in those physical ways in their little bodies, it blows my mind, and so that's when I made a deep connection with trust. It's not just theory, it's like, actual, actual reality for how it changes their bodies in their lives.

Then from there, it's like, okay, if my goal is to ultimately teach them this academic content, through our classroom community, through this sense of belonging, through, you know, this joyful experience, they have to trust me. So I have to be vulnerable, I have to lead with empathy, I have to show them that no matter what comes, because challenges will come just like they're guaranteed the challenges outside of my classroom, I say, we're going to face all of that as a classroom community. I am going to ebb and flow, I'm going to make mistakes, but I'm going to own up to those things, and they can trust that I am one of the adults that they can count on. Once they can count on me for that they can count on me to challenge them, to push them, to lean into the discomfort of learning that's their new asset, like all of that then becomes a part of our reality in our classroom. If trust is prioritized in the beginning, and then all the way throughout, right. . . .

One thing that I like to mention is that a lot of teachers think of like, building relationships as like, you do it early on, you know, it's fresh in a new school year, let's learn about each other, let's do the culture building, and then they drop it and then they're burnt out, December, January, February. As the year goes on, they get more and more burnt out, because they hold all the power all year, right and they never transfer that to students. Like, you have to be open with students that we're building this trust so that this trust evolves into leadership.

I'm going to start taking some steps back and let them know that that's part of trust, to let me know what I can expect from you. You can expect to transform and evolve into a leader here, in whatever way that works for you. It is my job to provide those opportunities for you to be able to showcase your brilliance in whatever way feels like it serves you, because that's what I want you to do with this learning. When you leave my classroom. I'm not teaching you for just this one year, I'm teaching you for a lifetime. So, whatever we learn, how will you use it? How can

(continued)

(continued)

you be a leader in this space with how you internalize this learning, and then we go there, but all that starts with trust in the beginning, and it'll evolve and grow and shift and change throughout the year. And that's the beautiful part about joyful learning, because you get excited about taking on challenges together. And no one's alone in that experience.

Individual Reflection/Collective Discussion:

1. What role did "trust" play in your experiences as a student going through your K–12 schooling? How, if at all, do you see aspects of your experiences playing out in what Alexia and Joscelyn share here?
2. In her reflections on trust, Joscelyn mentions that she is not teaching her students for the year, but for a lifetime. What life are you teaching your students for? In other words, what do you hope your students will know/believe about themselves and be able to do *beyond* the academic content? How does trust and vulnerability play into bringing that vision for your (future or current) *students* to life?

Conclusion

Inherent in the responses of all of the featured teachers in this chapter, teaching and learning are already rooted in risk-taking, and while teaching vulnerably is a powerful way of disrupting pre-existing power dynamics and social hierarchies, particularly those within dominant schooling structures, it is a process that must be navigated with care and caution *because* of these power dynamics and social hierarchies. For example, many educators who hold traditionally marginalized identities have found their sharing of their personal identities and narratives or authentic self-expressions punished, ridiculed, or used as a means to justify further marginalization as they're labeled as over-emotional, combative, or unprofessional. Additionally, perceptions of vulnerability as weakness can often hinder people's willingness to share openly due to fear of losing power, control, respect or otherwise negatively changing one's perception of them. In their exploration of teaching through vulnerability in the practice of preparing social workers, Gatwiri and Ife (2021) speak to and challenge this powerfully:

> Most people are raised to view vulnerability as a form of weakness. Those who are seen as strong are those who from the vantage point of others never seem "bothered" by emotions. Yet the numbing of vulnerability and the glorification of the "thick skin" ideology might be the root cause of the dysfunction in most professional and personal relationships. This is because, emotions cannot be numbed selectively and as such, numbing 'negative' emotions also numbs positive emotions and consequently hinder connection and change. (p. 9)

As covered numerous times throughout this book, many of us have internalized damaging narratives that who we are, the fullness of who we are, is both too much and not enough. Teaching and leading vulnerably disrupts this narrative acknowledging that if we are to truly build collaborative and collective learning environments rooted in trust, and supporting the kind of risk-taking that leads to deep connections and engagement with academic content, we must live, teach, and lead in the fullness of who we are.

REVISITING CRITICAL AUTOBIOGRAPHIES: Vulnerability

Return to your Critical Educational Autobiography, reflect on the following questions, and add the new information to the appropriate sections:

1. Reflecting on your own K–12 experiences, did you have any teachers who you felt allowed you to know and see them? If so, compare what it felt like to *be* and *learn* in their classes as compared to other teachers who perhaps didn't open up as much.
2. What messages did you internalize about vulnerability? How does that impact when and with whom you share certain aspects of who you are and your story? What comes up for you now as you think about what it might look and feel like for you to teach and lead vulnerably?
3. After reading this chapter, how has your understanding of the role and purpose of the educator changed or deepened?

References

Adams, C. M., & Forsyth, P. B. (2009). The nature and function of trust in schools. *Journal of School Leadership, 19*(2), 126–152.

Brantmeier, E. J. (2013). Pedagogy of vulnerability: Definitions, assumptions, and applications. In J. Lin, R. Oxford, & E. J. Brantmeier (Eds.), *Re-envisioning Higher Education: Embodied Pathways to Wisdom and Transformation* (pp. 95–106). Information Age Publishing.

Bryk, A., & Schneider, B. (2002). *Trust in schools: A core resource for improvement.* Russell Sage Foundation.

Darling-Hammond, L. (2006). Constructing 21st-century teacher education. *Journal of Teacher Education, 57*(3), 300–314. doi:10.1177/0022487105285962

Darling-Hammond, L. (2010). Teacher education and the American future. *Journal of teacher education, 61*(1–2), 35–47.

Emdin, C. (2011). Moving beyond the boat without a paddle: Reality pedagogy, black youth, and urban science education. *The Journal of Negro Education, 80*(3), 284–295.

Gatwiri, K., & Ife, J. (2023). Teaching about vulnerability and love in social work: lessons and reflections from two academics. *Social Work Education, 42*(3), 388–403.

Gay, G. (2018). *Culturally Responsive Teaching: Theory, Research, and Practice.* New York: Teachers' College Press.

Gay, G. (2005). Politics of multicultural teacher education. *Journal of Teacher Education, 56*(3), 221–228. doi:10.1177/0022487105275913

Irizarry, J. G. (2009). Representin': Drawing from hip-hop and urban youth culture to inform teacher education. *Education and Urban Society, 41*(4), 489–515. doi:10.1177/0013124508331154

Ladson-Billings, G. (1999). Preparing teachers for diverse student populations: A critical race theory perspective. *Review of Research in Education.* doi:10.2307/1167271

Ladson-Billings, G. (2005). Is the team all right? Diversity and teacher education. *Journal of Teacher Education, 56*(3), 229–234. doi:10.1177/0022487105275917

National Commission on Excellence in Education. (1983). A nation at risk: The imperative for educational reform. *The Elementary School Journal, 84*(2), 113–130.

Sleeter, C. E. (2000). Chapter 6: Epistemological diversity in research on preservice teacher preparation for historically underserved children. *Review of research in education, 25*(1), 209–250.

Smith, C. The danger of silence [Video]. TED. https://www.ted.com/talks/clint_smith_the_danger_of_silence?language=en

Chapter 7

Weaving Student Voice into Our Practice

Opening space for students to authentically engage in the creative processes of teaching and learning frees educators to engage their own creativity and passions as well.

Instagram Post
@drcourtneyrose (December 12, 2019)

In the process of humanizing education, the first step is humanizing ourselves as educators. It has been my observation that many teachers have a hard time seeing the humanity of their students within the educational spaces because they have been trained and conditioned not to see their own. As explored in Chapter 5, the cultural and political bodies of the "teacher" are often rooted in dehumanizing narratives that produce, support, and reward dehumanizing instructional policies and practices. The reflective activities and frameworks covered so far hopefully helped you to identify some of the ways you have both experienced, and perhaps, participated in your own dehumanization. In this chapter, I will extend those threads of our humanity to our students recognizing that one of the most powerful ways to acknowledge and honor our own humanity is to honor and acknowledge our students' humanity, and to collectively weave together space and opportunity for them to authentically express who they are and actively engage in processes of teaching and learning.

The Tangled Threads of Silence

During my doctoral studies, I stumbled across a video that was getting a lot of attention on the internet. The video was called "The Danger of Silence," and it featured a poem performed by poet, educator, scholar, and author of *How the Word Is Passed*, Dr. Clint Smith. In the poem, Smith shares how one year for Lent, he decided to give up his voice, but in the process realizes he'd done that a long time ago. He recounts various incidents where he did not speak up when he could and should have. There was the time when he saw students in the hall bullying another student for being gay, when he walked past a homeless man as if he was invisible, and when he said nothing after a woman praised him for working with his "poor, unintelligent" inner-city students. In his poem, Smith asks us to think about how our silence is often motivated by fear and the dangerous messages it sends to those on the receiving end. As an exclamation point to his argument, Smith offers this famous quote from Dr. Martin Luther King, Jr., "In the end, we will remember not the words of our enemies, but the silence of our friends." While you can't give your students voice, you can amplify and represent theirs in spaces they may not have access. Speak up in that faculty meeting, push back against that colleague in the teachers' lounge, and vote for policies that can change the landscape for students *and* teachers.

I agree with the sentiments at the root of Smith's poem and MLK, Jr's quote. However, reflecting on my own experiences as both a student and educator, I find that there are some narratives and practices of silence that are important to explore when determining how to create more engaging and empowering learning environments for both students and educators. A good place to start is to reflect on some of the dominant interpretations of silence. As Smith's poem explores, silence can be read as agreement and acceptance, which can be especially dangerous in matters of violence, inequity, and injustice. In those moments when we silently observe the dehumanization of others, we become complicit in it whether that is our intention or not. However, silence is also often read as discomfort, disagreement, or resistance, particularly as we find ourselves facing information or circumstances that challenge our perceptions of self and reality. In research exploring student attitudes in courses focusing on issues of diversity, race, and social inequity, this silence has been found to result in professors pulling back on digging deeply in the core issues of the courses, fearing that students may become resistant or unreceptive (Gorski, 2010; Lowenstein, 2005).

This brings me back to some of my own dissertation research and the ways silence played a role in how both the professor and the students experienced the hip-hop education course of focus. The professor, although admittedly bothered at times by the silence, had learned over time to read it, stating in his first interview:

> I've learned to read it. Like not all silence is discomfort, not all silence is violence, some silence is just "I'm thinking," and I've learned to read the faces of the students. There's probably one or two that I've read sometimes, you know, they *wanna* say something. . .and I'm like "It's okay you can be quiet you'll be alright," and there's some folks who are just deeply pondering and some folks who are making connections, but I've learned to read my students really, really well.

Here, the professor in the study expresses his understanding that there are also a variety of reasons that impact how, why, and when a student engages vocally in the class, if at all, which was supported by responses from participating students in their individual interviews.

When talking with in-service teacher Alicia and pre-service teacher Monica (two of the four Black participants), the topic of silence came up after Monica shared that she doesn't speak up much in the class, an observation I had already made in my own notes and memos. Alicia, who earlier in her individual interview stated that hip-hop culture "was just in [her]" having grown up in a community and social environment where hip-hop was the dominant lens, added on explaining why she did not speak very much in the class either:

> In [the hip-hop education class] in particular I don't feel like I need to say too much. A lot of the things I'm feeling are already said, whereas in my other courses I'm like y'all didn't talk about the Black kids, y'all didn't talk about the poor people so let me talk about it for you.

Alicia experienced the course as a space where she did not have to do the heavy lifting in ensuring that the topics that were often overlooked by her predominantly White classmates and professors in her other courses were covered. This is often a burden placed on students and professors of color who find themselves the one of a few, if not the only, person of color in most higher education settings making it easy for topics specific to the lived realities of impoverished, BIPOC populations untouched or inadequately covered. However, the hip-hop education course's framing through a hip-hop cultural lens inherently incorporated such topics, naturally building them in, leaving Alicia feeling free to sit quietly and soak in the information.

Other students provided additional reasons for not participating such as lack of confidence speaking up on specific hip-hop artists and practices and feeling more comfortable in general speaking in smaller groups than in whole group settings. For example, some students communicated discomfort with the structure, such as pre-service teacher Jasmine, who felt it just wasn't in her nature to jump into conversations and not wanting to share incorrect hip-hop knowledge. She, along with a few other participating teachers found the conversations were *too* dominated by those more comfortable with the *get in where you fit in* approach, leading to an imbalance of the professor's voice to students. However, most of the other participants walked away with deeper understandings of how opening up the discussion in a way that encouraged students to jump in where and how they felt comfortable not only built their knowledge and argumentation skills, but also built confidence in speaking up and against oppressive authority figures and systems that would hopefully carry into their interactions within their classrooms, schools, and communities at large.

Regardless of students' underlying reasons, silence, along with other nonverbal cues such as clapping and snapping, were considered acceptable ways to engage in the conversation. Once again this connects back to the traditional rules of engagement in the hip-hop cypher in which some participants assume the roles of audience members or hype people, whose claps, snaps, cheers, and general presence each time the cypher meets serve as valuable contributions to the performance, motivating and encouraging the rappers to continue, with the potential that, over time, they too may become comfortable enough to contribute a freestyle in the future (Emdin, 2013).

The preceding data provides a snapshot of the communal nature of the course's daily functioning through a deeper exploration of the weekly class discussions, or class cyphers. Rooted in the rules of engagement of the hip-hop cypher, the structure of the discussions stressed the *collective* perspectives and contributions of the *group* to develop deeper understandings of hip-hop culture and its potential as a pedagogical tool. Once again, this provided the enrolled teachers with the opportunity to learn *through* hip-hop pedagogy rather than *about* it, providing models through an immersive experience.

Similar dynamics play out in K–12 schools and classrooms. Historically marginalized groups often find it difficult to be heard and valued within schools that are built on a culture in which the social and cultural capital they enter with are not valued (Coleman, 1988; Lareau, 2007). Megan Boler's edited work *Democratic Dialogue in Education: Troubling Speech, Disturbing Silence* (2004) compiles essays of 10 authors exploring the possibility, strategies, and consequences of democratic dialogue within the classroom.

Boler's essay in the book presents an argument for what she calls "affirmative action pedagogy." According to Boler, this type of pedagogy "seeks to ensure that we bear witness to marginalized voices in our classrooms, even at the minor cost of limiting dominant voices" (p. 4). Acknowledging that all voices are not treated equally within schools, and society at large, Boler presents different examples of the methods in which educators act as allies in an attempt to raise the voices of the historically marginalized. This often occurs while simultaneously silencing the voices of the dominant group within the classroom setting to avoid instances of "hate speech" that would be harmful to the marginalized. In contrast, one of the other essays in the text, written by Cris Mayo, argues that the practice of silencing the oppressor only addresses the symptoms and does little to attack the *causes* of oppression harmful beliefs and actions. According to Mayo, silencing runs the risk of adding to the problem as "underlying attitudes and practices" leading to hateful speech are removed from open debate and fester beneath the surface.

These arguments are reminiscent of debates among various educational researchers on the issue of "colorblindness" or "racelessness." The goal of "racelessness" and "colorblindness" is to stop all talk of race to relieve tension and create a unified environment (Wells et al., 2005). However, while the silencing of all dialogue has the benefits on a surface level in that it acts as a preventative measure against possible racist attacks, it also closes opportunities to discuss the everyday racism that students of color feel as a result of policies and practices on the school, district, state, and national level (Fordham, 1991; Wells et al., 2005). Thus, the tension presented between Boler and Mayo early on in *Silenced Dialogue* over the issue of whether or not to silence the dominant group completely in an effort to hear the marginalized highlights the paradoxical effects of either choice.

Additionally, a second major theme of the book acts to complicate the issue even further exploring it from the opposite direction and questioning the benefits of embracing silence. Allison Jones begs the question of why dialogue or voice is seen as more valuable than silence. Presenting an argument that echoes those of sociologists and educational researchers such as Gloria Ladson-Billings (1996), Jones argues that silence is often used in an effort to resist feeding the "parasitic appetite" of the dominant group. According to Jones, the dominant group's inquiries into the experiences and emotions of the marginalized through forced dialogue across differences holds them in the position of power as the marginalized must "work" to make sure they are *heard*. Again, this opens up an issue of a paradoxical relationship where opening dialogue in the hopes of creating a feeling of understanding and equality creates, or recreates, a system of oppression and inferiority.

Similarly, professor of education, Huey-Li Li's essay in *Silenced Dialogue,* explores the benefits of using silence as a method of enhancing the learning experiences. In a society in which many often find silence uncomfortable, Li argues that silence can provide an opportunity for reflection and time to process not only what is being said, but also the manner in which it is said. These views on both embracing silence and forcing communication raise questions as to the most beneficial strategy for engaging in dialogue across differences in the classroom. Both the acts of forcing dialogue from students and/or silencing others can result in risky and traumatic experiences. Throughout the book, the authors are careful not to suggest that any one method works best in accomplishing these goals, as there are risks no matter what.

Overall, exploring the complexities and tangled threads of silence won't lead us to any *one* set of strategies that will work in *all* classrooms and learning environments. There are no "quick fixes," no "one size fits all" methods that an educator can walk away with in attempts to open up democratic dialogue within their own classroom and/or school. However, critically reflecting on how we have both interpreted silence, been silenced, and chosen to practice silence as both students and educators can help us to understand the role schools play in contributing to existing inequalities as well as the moral responsibility (and ability) that each individual educator has to effectively address this from the confines of our classrooms.

PAUSE, REFLECT, DISCUSS: To Be or Not to Be Silent

Considering some of the examples shared throughout this section, think of a time recently when you grappled with whether to speak up or remain silent. Reflect on and respond to the following questions. What is your final decision: to be or not to be silent? Explain.

- Whose peace, position, and/or power would your silence or lack of action protect? Whose does it disrupt or diminish?

(continued)

(continued)

- Whose voices, perspectives, realities, or needs would be amplified? Whose would be silenced or diminished?
- Could your speaking up or taking action cause additional harm to vulnerable or historically disenfranchised populations?
- What messages does your silence or lack of action send about where you sit on the issue? Does that message reflect your true feelings/position?
- Would speaking up or taking action fall in line with or push back against the status quo?
- Is the action you plan to take rooted in authentic desire for change or a self-serving display of performative or temporary solidarity?
- Are you remaining silent out of fear of how others will perceive you, particularly long-term friends and loved ones who sit in support of the injustice?

Increasing Student Voice

On the whole, student voice is a big topic in developing culturally relevant and humanizing practice. It's also one of the key areas that I focus on during my professional development sessions and in my teacher education courses. Talk and voice are often hyper-managed, and as a result, students can feel disconnected from the content and school/classroom community, pulling back from actively participating in the lessons as they either struggle or refuse to contort their voice to fit into the limited spaces created for them. Often, this particular practice of students' silence is misinterpreted as lack of care for and commitment to the learning process. Increasing opportunities for students to express their voices, as often and as authentically as possible, can reconnect them with the learning environment and academic content while also providing educators with useful insights into who they are and how to create the most effective learning environment for them.

The following are just a few suggestions of strategies that invite students to weave their voices, perspectives, and experiences into the teaching and learning process:

- **Student Journals:** This is a pretty common-sense one, and one that is probably most prevalent in classrooms today. Journals provide students with a space to reflect on key events in their personal and academic lives. The place where most teachers fall short is to engage in critical dialogue around how to connect the personal and academic experiences and utilize them to enhance their practice.
- **Student Art/Writing Walls:** For this one, I look to research specifically in the hip-hop education sphere that calls for a space for students to openly express themselves in written/artistic form. Give students a space to express themselves publicly. It will build their sense of ownership of the classroom environment, build confidence in their unique forms of self-expression, AND highlight talents that aren't often recognized or celebrated in the academic space.
- **Choice in Presenting Knowledge:** This is another one that's been around for a while, but can often get watered down in practice. If we want our students to be creative and critical thinkers, then we need to allow them the opportunity to do just that. Forcing them to choose from pre-selected options isn't really a choice. Provide students with the guidelines of what MUST be included, the topics and points they need to cover, some options for POTENTIAL approaches, and then let them fly.
- **Elicit Student Feedback:** I'm a HUGE proponent of this one, and I think it's actually gaining some steam in the K–12 setting. Ask your students for feedback on how the class is going and suggestions for improvement and ask for it often. They are your best source of professional development because THEY are who you're developing your practice for. Also break out of the survey. TALK with them. You'll gain MUCH deeper insight, and they can help you brainstorm new approaches and practices!

- **Engage in Non-academic Dialogue:** This one is at the core of all of the others. If all of the talk in your classroom or between you and your students is centered around academics, then it's lacking in depth. Our goal as educators is to attend to the WHOLE child and in order to do that we need to KNOW the whole child. Using some of the other methods listed here will help, but engage practices like critical dialogue circles or morning meetings to open up opportunities for non-academic talk where EVERYONE can get to know each other on a deeper level.

I have personally used *all* of these strategies at some point in my teaching career, both with my elementary school students and in my current practice as a professor. Of course, some strategies worked better than others and some worked with one group but not another group in the same grade or semester. The key was constantly engaging in cycles of collective reflection in which I opened myself up to real-time feedback from the students. For example, during the 2020–2021 academic year, I was teaching ALL of my face-to-face courses via Zoom and about a month into the course I realized that student participation and engagement in class discussions was dipping extremely low. After speaking with other colleagues and my TA, I realized that we all might be experiencing a bit of Zoom fatigue and decided to adjust the course schedule to allow students a week off from sitting in the Zoom room and engage with content via an online discussion board/journal activity instead. The journals/discussion board posts could be submitted as a written, video, or audio response and students could be as creative with their responses as they liked, but they still needed to make connections to *at least* one reading or video assigned in that particular section of the course. Almost immediately, I noticed class participation begin to sky rocket again. Upon reflection with the students they shared that the Zoom Break assignments not only gave them a much-needed break from hours sitting in front of their computers, but also opened up more time for them to engage with and reflect on course content so that they felt more confident and better prepared to share their thoughts in the class sessions. My TA and I kept refining the assignment throughout the semester, and taking their feedback, decided to make this a part of my courses moving forward. However, as we started to return to in-person courses, the participation in the online discussion boards actually began to feel like *more* work to the students in the in-person section of the same course and as a group we decided to cut the discussion boards, and instead engage in some sort of in-class discussion or review of the literature in small and whole group formats. The lesson learned here: Consistently enacting practices that affirm and engage students' voices will always result in more productive and positive learning environments. Stay the course and trust the process.

Weaving Together Academic and Cultural Identities

During my teacher preparation program, and even more so during my time with Teach For America, creating engaging hooks to bring students into our lessons was a key practice in developing our lesson planning skills. As culturally relevant pedagogy was growing increasingly popular and gaining widespread attention within teacher preparation, we were encouraged to either insert our own interests or the students' interests to create student buy-in and increase engagement with academic content. However, these hooks were often quickly abandoned as teachers moved into the direct instruction and core content of the subjects. Using cultural artifacts and practices as hooks to traditional instructional approaches reels students in, but often results in tossing back valuable pieces of their identities. Rather than this bait and switch tactic, teachers who aim to produce more engaging educational experiences should construct lessons that function as bridges instead, allowing students to move freely between their personal, social, and academic identities as they authentically engage with the academic content.

The key shortcoming of the lesson hook approach was the misguided belief that in order for a lesson to be effective, meaningful, and engaging *all* it needed to be is fun and exciting. I am certainly an advocate for joy, fun, and excitement as core components of a classroom community. Whether it was back when I was an elementary school teacher or in my work as a professor, my classrooms were filled with music, movement, laughter, and high energy and emotion. However, I also recognize and deeply believe that deep engagement and identification with the learning process might not always feel or look like a party. Honestly speaking, many of the greatest and most meaningful learning experiences, the ones that pushed me deeper into myself and revealed my power and strength, were as far from what one might define as "fun" and "exciting" as possible. They were, however, deeply connected to who I was, who I hoped to become, and driven by my own personal passions, and interests. As educators, focusing too much on rooting our practice in fun learning experiences might produce students who enjoy the learning process, and again, enjoyment is something we should strive for as often as possible. However, focusing on rooting our instruction in the development of inclusive, affirming, and sustaining learning environments, which may not always bring "fun" to the surface of our students' minds, will produce students who *identify* with the learning process.

The use of hooks also sent the message that things students most deeply connected and identified with were only valuable in certain times in the learning process, a message that was deeply reinforced when they were abandoned once the lesson was in full swing. Ultimately, as educators, almost everything that we do within our practice communicates messages to our students, explicitly and implicitly, about what is valuable, desirable, smart, good, and so on. Even when well-intentioned, the impacts of some of our practices aimed at equipping students to successfully navigate schooling and society beyond our classrooms can have detrimental impacts on how they see themselves and others around them. For students of color, those living in impoverished communities and/or at the intersections of historically marginalized identities, these practices can also lead to shifting views and relationships with members of their own families and communities as they begin to prioritize and privilege the cultural ways of knowing and being prioritized and privileged within the culture of schooling and society at large.

In his most notable text, *Pedagogy of the Oppressed* (1996), Brazilian philosopher, educator and author, Paulo Freire, outlines what he sees as the cornerstone of an oppressive educational system, the narrative created through the implementation and framing of education as a *banking concept*.

In this conceptualization of education, students are framed as empty receptacles into which teachers deposit information, and in Freire's analysis, the more completely a teacher is able to fill their receptacles, the more effective they are in the eyes of the system and society. According to Freire, the banking concept of education mirrors oppressive society as it relies on the following attitudes and practices:

- The teacher teachers and the students are taught.
- The teacher knows everything and the students know nothing.
- The teacher thinks and the students are thought about.
- The teacher talks and the students listen—meekly.
- The teacher disciplines and the students are disciplined.
- The teacher chooses and reinforces his choice, and the students comply.
- The teacher chooses the program and the students have the illusion of acting through the actions of the teacher.
- The teacher confuses the authority of knowledge with his or her own professional authority, which she and he sets in opposition to the freedom of the students.
- The teacher is the subject of the learning process, while the students are mere objects. (Freire, 1996)

Freire's exploration of the banking model provides a useful framework through which to analyze how traditional and dominant policies and practices within K–12 public education are often subtractive, requiring that students change or shed pieces of their authentic selves in order to assimilate into the culture of schooling, rather than additive that would utilize these aspects of their identities to foster deeper and more comprehensive engagement with the learning materials. The chart, *Subtractive Approaches versus Additive Approaches,* breaks down the differences between additive and subtractive approaches, and how they can sever the ties between students' home/family community, and ultimately, their sense of self.

SUBTRACTIVE APPROACHES VERSUS ADDITIVE APPROACHES	
Subtractive	**Additive**
– **Replace** students' diverse cultural ways of knowing and being with those of dominant society	+ Use students' diverse cultural ways of knowing and being as **tools to build** their own cultural and social capital
– Cultural differences viewed as **hindrances and barriers** to the educational process and academic success	+ Cultural differences are viewed as **assets** to the educational process and in achieving academic success
– Can **weaken family & community ties** as students are pushed to let go of their home cultures	+ **Maintains or strengthens family & community ties** as they are integrated in the teaching and learning process
– Negatively impacts identity development and **compartmentalization of cultural, social, & academic identities**	+ Promotes positive identity development and **fusion of cultural, social, & academic identities**

PAUSE, REFLECT, DISCUSS

1. After reviewing the additive versus subtractive approaches, reflect on whether the majority of your own K–12 experiences were rooted in additive or subtractive approaches. Provide specific examples when possible and explore how these approaches impacted your perceptions of yourself, your community, and your family throughout your educational journey.
2. Currently practicing educators: Reflect on one or more areas in your practice that is clearly rooted in subtractive approaches (i.e., math instruction). Reflect on how you can reconstruct the practice so that it is more firmly rooted in an additive approach.

Valuing Students in the Learning Process

What would happen if we prepared teachers to create classrooms in which students felt *valued* rather than comfortable? I posed this question to pre-service teachers enrolled in my section of the Teaching Diverse Populations course. As educators, we definitely want our students to feel safe and comfortable in our classrooms. However, sometimes pushing for safety and comfort begs the questions:

1. Whose safety and comfort are we prioritizing?
2. Whose voices, experiences, identities, perspectives, and cultural ways of knowing and being are we silencing or overlooking in the name of safety and comfort?

These questions came front and center in my own home state as policies in Florida pushed to ban books and other instructional materials that have been found to cover topics associated with a theoretical framework known as critical race theory (CRT), causing discomfort and concern amongst various parent, teacher, and student populations. In the bill, referred to by the governor as the STOP W.O.K.E. Act (actual name: Individual Freedom in Education), there is a clause that states: *A person should not be instructed that he or she must feel guilt, anguish, or other forms of psychological distress for actions, in which he or she played no part, committed in the past by other members of the same race or sex.* Proponents of the bill argued that they are protecting the mental and emotional health of students who are either made to feel as though they are to blame for the acts of those in the past or taught that they are inherently oppressed or oppressor. Opponents of the bill argued that although the language of the bill seems protective of students' learning experiences, its true intention is to encourage further erasure of identities, historical events, and experiences through a watered-down version of our nation's history.

These concerns seemed to come to fruition during the 2022–2023 school year as the Florida State Department of Education (FLDOE) rejected the implementation of an Advanced Placement (AP) African American History course claiming that it directly violated the STOP W.O.K.E. Act due to its coverage of critical race theory through instruction on intersectionality and queer theory, two components that those who developed and piloted the course note were minor, and optional, components of the course. In a letter written to the College Board, the organization through which all AP courses are developed, piloted, and governed, FL Department of Education stated that, as written, the course lacked in educational value, which many educators, parents, and students felt sent a very clear message about how much the FLDOE values the African American students, teachers, parents, and communities it serves. The Stop W.O.K.E. bill and subsequent policies, including the rejection of the AP African American History course, serve as powerful examples of what can happen when we overlook minor exclusionary and subtractive policies and approaches within schools.

Student-Driven Classroom Management

One key area where many teachers, particularly new teachers, have issues is with classroom management. Again, incorporating student voice and engaging students in the creative processes of the class management plan and daily functioning of the space can go a long way in addressing some of these issues. I don't often teach methods courses, but during my first job as an adjunct professor, I was asked to revamp and teach the institution's classroom management for secondary educators' course in which the culminating project was a comprehensive classroom management plan. One of the things that I had my students do is to create their classroom management statement of purpose. If you've ever developed a classroom management plan as a part of a teacher education program, then you know the statement of purpose goes at the top, and viewing samples online, they're usually about two to three sentences long and say something pretty generic like: *the purpose of this classroom management plan is to develop a classroom environment that feels safe and welcoming, and will encourage students to engage and learn.*

Many people rooted in student-driven, culturally responsive approaches have expanded on this, and I also adapted a practice with my students in which they write a much more extensive statement of purpose that covers four aspects of classroom management and their classroom management philosophy. The first component asks them to explore their beliefs about students and poses questions such as:

- Do you think that students should be controlled or that students should be disciplined or that they can be taught to be self-controlled and can manage themselves?
- Do you think that students are naturally disruptive or do you think that some of their behaviors that are deemed as disruptive or undesirable may just be different, or the ways that they are authentically engaging, and that those behaviors can be leveraged to enhance the classroom environment?

The second component asks teachers to explore their beliefs about the teacher's role, posing the following questions:

- Is it in your belief that the teacher's role is to be the boss and to run that space completely or that the teacher should be more of a guide? Why do you believe that?
- Should the teacher be a facilitator or should you be the control center?
- What's your view on creating rules? Should that be a collaborative process or should that be something that a teacher does on their own?

The third component focuses on teachers' beliefs about managing a classroom and poses the following questions:

- Do you believe in establishing an authoritarian, permissive, or democratic environment? What would that look like and why do you feel that way? How would each of those lend themselves to developing the type of classroom environment that you want to have?
- What constitutes disruptive behavior and what's just excitement about learning or energetic engagement in the academic process? How do you differentiate between disruption and excitement?

- What does a well-managed classroom look like to you, and is that more deeply rooted in your cultural and educational backgrounds? Do you think your students see that the same way? Why or why not?

The last area is beliefs about community and communication, particularly with students' parents/caretakers, which we dig into much deeper in the following chapter.

- How do you plan on communicating and getting to know your students? How do you plan on getting to know their parents and families?
- What do you think your students' families feel is the best way to get to know and communicate with them?
- How do you envision your students' parents/families/caregivers being a part of your classroom environment? What role(s) do you hope they play and how will you help facilitate that?

Collectively, these questions require that teachers critically reflect on how they feel about how effective classroom management and positive classroom engagement looks and feels. When I facilitate this process with pre-service teachers, I ask them to think about how deeply their beliefs are rooted in their very specific cultural norms and their very specific educational background and how that might differ from, and potentially cause tension between, the community of students, teachers, parents, and families that they may work for and with. Similar to what happens in the exploration of the critical autobiography, engaging in the development of this incredibly thorough statement of purpose creates a greater sense of awareness about how the ways that the teachers are thinking about classroom management, the practices that they think they should enact, speak more to what *they* connect with and what is meaningful and effective for *them*, than what might be meaningful and effective for their students. As educators, we're developing a space that we will share *with* our students, and if we don't engage in this process of thinking about how what we're doing might be more conducive to *our* learning versus their learning, then we've already missed the mark. When we develop a culturally responsive mindset, rooted in student-driven approaches that then manifests into a culturally responsive, student-driven learning environment, we shift the entire culture of the classroom to one that is not only more liberating, more welcoming, more engaging for the students, but it's also more liberating, more engaging, more welcoming for us as the educator because we're shifting from something that is rooted in the singular perspective of one individual, which is me the educator, to one that is more collaborative and communal, which invites all of our voices and all of our experiences into the space. When we can open that up and share that responsibility with our students, and even invite their families/caretakers into the process, we create a more communal environment, and hopefully, a space that is much less restrictive for everyone. It's a shift that has the potential to open up so many more opportunities for collaboration between all of the key stakeholders involved in a students' educational journey. I always remind teachers that a lot of the practices that feel restrictive and limiting to our students also leave us in a position as educators to feel very restricted and limited. I mean, we've all complained or have had our thoughts about having to have very scripted, very canned, very normalized, very hyper-structured approaches to instruction, right? Featured teachers Joscelyn, Alexia, Brian, and Jeff speak to some of the student-driven approaches they've woven into their classrooms over the years and the impacts that had on the overall culture and climate of their classroom communities.

FEATURED TEACHERS: Student-Driven Practice

Joscelyn

It made them [the students] see what is possible, through the prism of what I was creating in that classroom. This is an adult, who cares deeply about our learning, but she's involved in the learning with us. And she wants to learn about us and she wants to use our lives as the content that

(continued)

(continued)

we teach. So it was more about transformation, through their stories and their lives, and how they will see the learning outside of my classroom, then this transfer of information, which removes identity. So the only way we see students using academic content, is to transform it into a way that resonates and is relatable for them. Because, then they will fall back on that, like, oh, I learned that from Ms. Reed, or that is like, something I talked to Ms. Reed about, or something I talked to my classmate about. And I am seeing this over here in the grocery store, I am seeing this in the barber shop, or I am talking to my family about it. That is the bigger picture as well. Big picture teaching is like, if it doesn't connect to your outside world, it is not worth doing it in the classroom. Right? Because it's gonna go in one ear and out the other. That is not what is going to matter in their grand scheme of their educational experience. So it is not an option.

Alexia

This year, I would really try to revamp how I did my classroom, like I have always had. . .freedoms and giving them [students] choice and everything that they do, but this time, I took a back seat, and I changed my role. So I made them more of the teachers and I took a back seat. So they run the classroom, basically as a society. . .how we would want society to look. They are kind of doing it.

So from leading in the morning. . .of course, you have to model those things. But now, we have our DJ of the day, who runs the entire classroom. We have their affirmations that they lead from the start of the day, our morning meeting where they incorporate us. I try my best to incorporate those, just the language and, and different skills and strategies on how to communicate, how to show integrity, all the different things for the SEL [social emotional learning] but we have been doing that all along. And so they get to share a part of their life and share how they are feeling and how they cope and deal with it. So I really want to make them the center of everything that we do. And then that trickles into, how we even take care of the classroom, how we speak to one another, what do you enjoy doing? How can I incorporate that into our lessons in our work? Even for academic reasons. They lead our meetings and our sessions with freedom and choice.

Brian

I think that if we work collectively and if our children recognize that there is no "I" just because I am the teacher, or because I am the leader, or because I am the principal or vice principal, but this is a "we." This is a collective piece that I am because we are that you are because you know who your ancestors were. And this whole idea of collective work and responsibility is something that is so ingrained, that it is hard for me to say because even though I share that I am a spiritual being, and I am a creative being, my creativity and my spiritual, formation is locked into the creativity and the spiritual formation of our bodies. And so, it is hard for me to say, "This is who I am." And that is how I incorporate it. Because it is a collaborative effort. That is really the spirit of Ubuntu. When we think about our ancestors and our ancestral lineage and legacy, yep, it was a whole understanding of we and we. . .because we oftentimes have been forced to bifurcate the wheat to separate the we from the I. We now live in a space where we only are focusing on I. Yeah. It is always this collective effort, right? There is no individual response and responsibility, but it is this collective effort that helps us to achieve what it is that we are trying to achieve. Yeah. And if we don't walk in that space, or if we just talk about it, and do not walk in that space, then we will not achieve it and walking in that space means even in the way you speak. Right?

Jeff

So, yeah, that is how, by knowing that it is not about me. I have worked with teachers and I work with teachers, who were some of the most brilliant people I have ever met, as far as the material, whether it is calculus, algebra, geometry, whatever, just ridiculously brilliant people that could not teach. Because when they looked at the material, they just looked at

(continued)

(continued)

it. How can you not see this? It is so easy. It is obvious. It is not obvious. It is not about how you see it. It is about how they [students] see it. Yeah. And so if they cannot see it, you have to be able to find a way to help them see it their way, not your way. You try your way, and then my work, it is gonna work for what I'm presenting to people, but then there is still going to be a big percentage that it is not going to work for. So then you have to find out, okay, well, that didn't work for them. How about this? That will work for another percentage and okay, you still have to whittle down to get to 0%. It is about them. It is about bringing those students, your students in, focusing on what they need, and their trades and their skills and their passions and all that stuff. You know, that's how you can be successful.

Reflecting on these comments from our featured teachers pushed me to reflect on some of the ways I slowly incorporated more student-driven practices into my own practice as a K–12 educator. I taught fifth grade math and science so there were a lot of manipulatives around; we had computer stations and lots of hands-on activities going on simultaneously throughout the day. I wanted my students to feel free to get up and use whatever materials they needed to help them to engage in the particular learning experience we had going on. As the teacher, I don't know what each individual child needs at all times, and students should feel like they have the freedom to go get the material that they need in order to fully engage with the learning process. One of the things that I really didn't monitor as much as some of the other teachers did was restriction of movement because a child might need to stand to really get into this lesson on fractions that I'm teaching or during our conversation about different types of clouds, a child might need to get up and go look at the clouds outside the window. When educators develop these student-driven, culturally responsive mindsets, that center community, collaboration, and bi-directional dialogue, it puts so much less pressure on the educator's head because the classroom community is working together as a unit to move forward. I've shared this many times and one of the responses I often get is teachers telling me if they had this sort of policy, their students would likely abuse it and chaos would ensue.

This leans back into the discussion of trust from Chapter 6. Enacting student-driven practices *requires* that we root our classroom community in radical trust and belief that our students know what they need and when we create space for them to communicate and access the things they need, we can trust them not to "abuse" that, for lack of a better word, power. Isn't our job as educators, after all is said and done, to empower our students to advocate for themselves, both inside and outside of the classroom? How can they do this if all we've taught them to do is ask permission to access what they need because the world doesn't trust that they won't "behave" as the world wants them to. Now of course, as was discussed in Chapter 6, this requires some dialogue, lots of consistency and trial and error. Did my students occasionally test the waters? Of course—they're kids and humans, it's just bound to happen. But my students knew that when they broke the trust we'd built together, when they crossed the boundaries that WE set together as a class, we were going to have some discussions and likely make some changes. But I involved them, and sometimes, yes, their parents/caretakers, every step of the way. The classroom wasn't *mine*. I set the tone, I took the lead of reinforcing the norms we'd set and holding each other accountable, but eventually they began to step up in this regard as well because I trusted and *believed* they could.

Conclusion

A lot of the pre-service teachers enrolled in my courses often took my classes on developing student-driven practices and would come out thinking "Okay, I took the class so now I'm culturally responsive." To that I say, maybe some of them were right, maybe they came in a bit further along in their understanding of the process or maybe a really transformational shift has happened over the course of the semester. However, one of the things that somebody with a student-driven, culturally responsive mindset understands is that you are not working toward some predetermined point of arrival. They operate, instead, with an understanding that they are going to be constantly in development. Maxine Greene writes about the concept of *becoming*, and the student-driven culturally responsive educator knows and understands that they are in a constant *state of becoming* because they're always going to have a different set of students who bring new challenges, new cultural expectations, new cultural backgrounds, new cultural understandings. They recognize that they themselves, with every interaction and engagement and experience that they have, are going to develop new understandings, new interpretations, new cultural frames of reference, Finally, they understand the fact that we're all teaching within a society and within a system that is constantly shifting and changing, requires that we constantly shift and change to respond. Remember, the operative word in culturally responsive is the word *responsive*. As educators, we are constantly in a state of responding. Once the initial practice of the self-work and reflecting on past experiences, the norms that you carry with you, is complete, you begin to develop this practice of engaging and communicating on a more *communal* level with your students, with other teachers maybe, and definitely with parents, families, and important cultural community members to help you to develop something that's more effective for not you but your students. Then you recognize that it has to be a continuous process of identifying the norms and practices, communicating and collaborating with parents, families, and students and other teachers and community members, enacting those practices that you've co-constructed with these members of your learning community and evaluating the effectiveness, right? This is not a point of arrival, it is a constant process of development, and that is the belief that must lie at the core of any student-driven practices.

REVISITING CRITICAL AUTOBIOGRAPHIES: Your Student-Driven Practice

Return to your Critical Educational Autobiography, reflect on the following questions, and add the new information to the appropriate sections:

1. Reflecting on your own K–12 experiences, do you think you had instruction that was rooted more in *additive* or *subtractive* practices? Give examples. How did this impact your development of your *academic identity* and your vision for yourself as an educator?
2. What messages did you internalize about how silence operates in the learning environment? How, if at all, have you either seen or used silence as a tool in creating change? Do you actually think this is an effective approach, why or why not?
3. Review the Culturally Relevant Classroom Management Plan instructions in Appendix 4. Spend time writing your expanded statement of philosophy. How does it align and overlap with some of what you touched on in your original critical autobiography? For currently practicing educators, pose some of the questions about their conceptions of a well-managed classroom to your students. Review and discuss your responses with each other and identify points of alignment and misalignment. Collectively brainstorm ways to address some of the major areas of disagreement or misalignment.

References

Apple, M. W. (1971). The hidden curriculum and the nature of conflict. *Interchange 2*(4), 27–40.

Boler, M. (Ed.). (2004). *Democratic Dialogue in Education: Troubling speech, Disturbing Silence.* New York: Peter Lang Publishing.

Coleman, J. S. 1998. Social capital in the creation of human capital. *American Journal of Sociology 94*, 95–120.

Emdin, C. (2013). The rap cypher, the battle, and reality pedagogy: Developing communication and argumentation in urban science education. In M. L. Hill & E. Petchauer (Eds.), *Schooling Hip-Hop: Hip-Hop based education across the curriculum*. New York: Teachers College Press.

Freire, P. (1996). *Pedagogy of the Oppressed* (revised). New York: Continuum, 356, 357–358.

Fordham, S. (1991). Racelessness in private schools: Should we deconstruct the racial and cultural identity of African-American adolescents? *Teachers College Record, 92*(3), 470–484.

Gorski, P. C. (2010). The scholarship informing the practice: Multicultural teacher education philosophy and practice in the U.S. *International Journal of Multicultural Education, 12*(2). doi:10.18251/ijme.v12i2.352

Greene, M. (1978). Teaching: The question of personal reality. *Teachers College Record, 80*(1), 24–35.

Greene, M. (1993). Diversity and inclusion: Toward a curriculum for human beings. *Teachers College Record, 95*(2), 211–221.

Ladson-Billings, G. (1996). Silence as weapons: Challenges of a black professor teaching white students. *Theory into Practice, 35*(2), 79–85.https://doi.org/10.1080/00405849609543706

Lareau, A. (2007). Unequal childhoods. In M. L. Andersen & P. Hill Collins (Eds.), *Race, Class, and Gender: An Anthology* (pp. 348–358). Belmont, CA: Thomson.

Lowenstein, K. L. (2009). The work of Multicultural teacher education: Reconceptualizing white teacher candidates as learners. *Review of Educational Research, 79*(1), 163–196. doi:10.3102/0034654308326161

Wells, A. S., Holme, J. J., Revilla, A. T., & Atanda, A. K. (2005). How desegregation changed us: The effects of racially mixed schools on students and society. *Columbia University*. https://www.tc.columbia.edu/articles/2004/march/how-desegregation-changed-us-the-effects-of-racially-mixed-/

Chapter 8

Collaborating with Parents, Families, and Communities

The continued teachers versus parents blame game is so exhaustingly counterproductive. Parents & Educators, we are NOT each other's enemies, and until we humanize each other and begin to value & respect what BOTH sides bring to the table, our children will continue to lose.

Twitter/Instagram Post
@drcourtneyrose (February 10, 2023)

One of the core memories that sticks out from my first year as a Lead Teacher of my own fifth-grade class was the Meet the Teacher night. This was a night late in the week before the first day of school when all of the students came to campus with their parents to, you guessed it, meet their teacher(s) for the coming year. I was so incredibly nervous for this event because I didn't know what to expect from my students' parents. Although I'd already spent some time working in classrooms and communicating with parents as an assistant teacher and definitely had my fair share of parent interactions during my *many* years as a self-proclaimed professional summer camp counselor, this felt very different. I was going to be the sole, or primary, adult responsible for the care, safety, and education of, to use Lisa Delpit's words, *other people's children*, and no matter how much I thought I knew about teaching, I knew their parents/caretakers held keys to reaching their children that no amount of reading, observations, and classroom experience could provide.

Throughout my years in the classroom I always knew that it was important to nurture the relationship with my students' parents/caregivers. Our parents and families are our first educators, and for most, our biggest champions and most committed advocates. The necessity for partnerships between families and schools is heavily documented, with stronger relationships associated with improved academic performance, more positive behavior both at home and school, and strong social skills. School-family partnerships also improve overall school climate, leading to greater support systems and networks to alleviate stress for both families and educators. Given all of this, it's clear why so many schools and districts prioritize building strong relationships and partnerships with families, but the data also shows that, nationwide, fostering consistently positive and productive relationships with parents/caregivers is often one of the hardest goals to reach.

As with any relationship, navigating conflict is a key factor that will either strengthen or weaken the ability to develop a positive and productive partnership. Considering that today's educators and schools are serving a rapidly diversifying population of students, families, and communities, it is expected that differing perspectives on "good teaching" and "good parenting" will arise, causing rifts in the family/teacher relationship. As conflicts between parents/families and educators/schools have resulted in a seemingly never-ending blame game that consistently places one group against the other.

Critically Reflecting on Internalized Beliefs about Family Involvement

So much of how we think about how parents/families should be involved in students' learning is informed not only by what we've read in the research but what we experienced, or didn't experience, in our own families. Through critically reflecting on your own parents'/families' engagement throughout your K–12 schooling experiences and the messages you internalized about yourself and them through that, you can begin to weave together the internalized messages you may have about "good," "bad," "positive," "negative" family involvement/engagement *and* teaching. However, as with any critical reflection, the most important component is to reflect on who certain narratives prioritize and privilege, who they afford greater access to opportunities/resources/experiences, and who they leave out. As I often tell my pre- and in-service teachers, critical reflection provides an opportunity to look for patterns, to connect dots, and see things with greater clarity and complexity. So as you reflect on these experiences, think about the things you wish your teachers knew about *why* your parents/caregivers engaged or didn't engage with your schooling in certain ways, and how that might have changed your academic experience and development of your academic identity. Before continuing with the rest of this chapter, take a moment to complete (and discuss with classmates, colleagues, and/or critical friends, if possible) the following reflection questions.

PAUSE, REFLECT, DISCUSS: Views on Family Involvement/Engagement

1. What is/are the role(s) of parents/families/caregivers during a child's K–12 educational experience? In other words, what does "good parenting" look like to you when it comes to engagement and involvement in their child's schooling?
2. Discuss some key experiences in your *own* K–12 schooling that may have shaped and informed these beliefs.
3. How might these beliefs about parent/family/caregiver involvement be rooted in your own cultural norms/practices/beliefs about schooling and education?
4. In what ways do you see these beliefs showing up in your own engagement with *your* children's teachers and/or with *your* students' parents/families/caregivers?

Cultural Barriers

In her book *Other People's Children: Cultural Conflict in the Classroom*, scholar and author, Lisa Delpit, provides multiple examples of how the deficit-based lens through which many communities of color and impoverished communities are viewed can create *cultural barriers* between schools and families. In one particularly poignant example, she takes us to a predominantly Latiné school in Boston where teachers became frustrated with the mothers of first-grade students because they kept bringing them to class prior to the bell ringing. The teachers wanted the parents to leave the children on the playground with the teachers' aides so that they could prepare their classrooms for the day. Becoming increasingly frustrated that the mothers continued to bring the children into the classrooms, the teachers resorted to locking the school doors, which resulted in yelling matches between the parents and teachers, and ultimately, the parents filed a complaint with the school board. As Delpit explains, there was a simple solution right in the teachers' grasp if they'd only taken the time to *speak* with the mothers:

> What the teachers in this instance did not understand was that the parents viewed six-year-olds as still being babies and in need of their mother's or their surrogate mother's (the teacher's) attention. To the parents, leaving children outside; without one of their "mothers" present was tantamount to child abuse and exhibited a most callous disregard for the children's welfare. The situation did not have to have become so highly charged. All that was needed was some knowledge about the parents and community of the children they were teaching, and the teachers could have resolved the problem easily—perhaps by stationing one of the first-grade teachers outside in the mornings, or by inviting one of the parents to remain on the school grounds before the teachers called the children in to class. (2006, p. 176)

This powerful example from Delpit sheds light on how unexplored biases and assumptions rooted in deficit-based frameworks can actually lead to the misinterpretation of the culturally-specific ways that parents and families love, care for, and protect their children. These teachers, so much more concerned with upholding rigid expectations, even missed the deep reverence and trust their students' mothers had for *them* as they referred to them as their "surrogate mothers." When we continue to frame and view anything *different* as inherently *lacking* or *wrong*, we close off opportunities to engage in meaningful dialogue, to reach deeper levels of understanding, and to create collaborative partnerships that actually resolve conflicts rather than amplify them.

This story also sheds light on the core issue that has consistently positioned parents/caretakers as *barriers* to enacting effective instruction for students: *who should have a stronger role in raising America's children?* As discussed in Chapter 2, part of the push for a more widely accessible education system was to protect democracy and the nation's future by preparing America's youth with the "proper" knowledge, skills, and moral compass, a task many of America's parents were not trusted to do properly. Over time, as the public education system, and the society around it, has evolved and diversified, debates continuously arise about how involved parents should be in the decision-making processes relevant to their children's education.

The 14th Amendment gives parents the right to make decisions about the *type* of schooling environment they think is going to be most effective for their child, disrupting the initial compulsory nature of American schooling that required all students to attend a public school. Reform efforts rooted in school choice have continued to build on these rights by providing parents with more options and even funding through vouchers and the like to mitigate costs of sending their children to private schools or even charters that may result in the family incurring additional fees. This emphasis on parent voice by way of choice is simultaneously praised and critiqued as it creates a sense of competition that some feel push educators in *all* schools (public, private, charter, etc.) to hold themselves accountable to providing the highest quality education they can for their enrolled and potential students. However, others note that it creates a false narrative that unfairly blames teachers for the inequitable experiences that some students face in schools, draining resources and support from the public schooling system, and leaving those for whom choosing another school is not feasible in even worse conditions.

One of the activities that I often have both pre- and in-service teachers do is to think about the way that decision-making power flows within our nation's education system. For the most part we end up with a flow chart that looks like Figure 8.1.

Now, in Figure 8.1, based on a conversation that I had in one of my spring 2023 courses, the parents have the same level of power, or fall in the same level as the school board. My students had a very hard time figuring out where to place parents because, in effect, they felt that similar to teachers, parents often found themselves at the mercy of the decision-making taking place by others higher in the chain of command, like the school board and the superintendent. However, they also noted that many times the positions on these boards are held *by* members of the community who have or at one time had students in the schools so they hold a dual role.

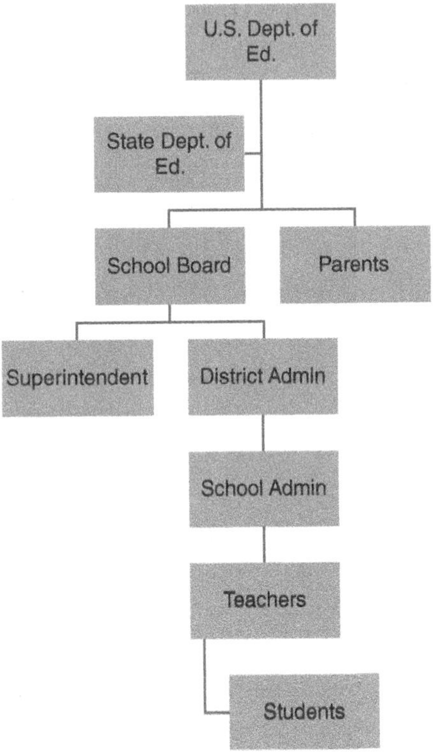

Figure 8.1 Decision-Making Power Flow within our Nation's Education System.

In another one of my courses, our discussion produced a similar, but slightly different, image that placed parents much more in line with teachers, shown in Figure 8.2.

The students in this section of my course felt that the debates that often arose about both teacher and parent voice in the decision-making processes about what should be covered in schools and how left them both in the same positions of power. They also felt that this was likely the reason why these sorts of tensions were emphasized and often exacerbated by politicians vying for votes. We saw this play out leading up to both the 2020 and 2024 elections as liberal candidates largely ran on teacher-centered platforms pushing for greater pay for teachers and more explicit support and valuing of their expertise. Conservatives on the other hand ran

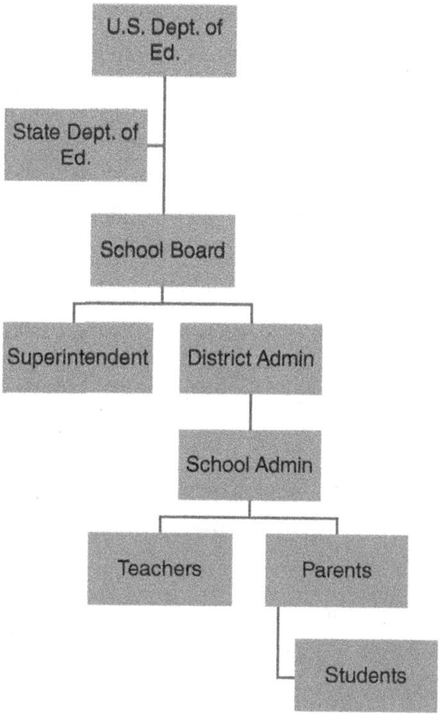

Figure 8.2 Modified Decision-Making Power Flow within Our Nation's Education System.

on platforms that largely claimed to push for greater parental rights as they targeted instructional practices and materials that they felt were indoctrinating students rather than educating them.

Some of these practices and materials were covered in Chapters 3 and 7 with the censorship of how America's history with race and racism is discussed and taught in schools in certain states (i.e., Florida and Texas where anti-critical race theory bills were passed between 2021 and 2023). An additional area of focus is on any formal instruction, materials, or policies that explicitly address gender and sexual identities. Again, debates ensued over whose responsibility it is to cover these issues in the collective raising and educating of America's children. What makes this conversation especially alarming is the false narrative they create that positions all, or the majority of, teachers as all holding one position and all, or most, parents standing in opposition of that. In actuality, educators *and* parents/caretakers fall all along the spectrum. Parents/caretakers showed up to school board meetings in support of teachers (and students) to protest the district and statewide policies banning books and topics from being taught. Likewise, teachers showed up to similar meetings in support of parent/family groups and community organizations arguing *for* these policies and raising concerns about specific materials being used in various grade levels. This false narrative has continued to fuel a politically charged educational climate in which students, teachers, *and* parents are used as political pawns in a game that often puts folks holding the most vulnerable identities at the greatest risk.

Given this, many districts have tried to employ strategies that will foster more authentic dialogue between families and educators, particularly in communities where the potential for large cultural differences between home and school culture may exist. One such approach that is taking rise in many districts across the country is the teacher home visit, which is intended to bridge home and school cultures by bringing teachers *to* the families. However, with opponents of the practice noting many potential pitfalls, this is a practice that must be employed with great attention to detail in order to ensure it does not actually reproduce and reinforce deficit-based beliefs.

The Complexities of Home Visits

The summer after my third year teaching fifth grade, I served as a corps member advisor in one of Teach For America's (TFA) summer institutes. It was my second summer serving in this role, but for the first time the organization opened some smaller institutes in certain regions where they would only have the incoming TFA teachers, referred to as corps members, assigned to that region. In the traditional model they sent multiple regions' incoming corps to the same city, with an attempt to align academic calendars, demographics of students, and overall culture and context in which the corps members would serve. These smaller institutes were opened to promote more specific development around the particular issues a given region faced as well as the ability to strengthen partnerships with the community and leverage as much expertise for current corps members and alumni in the area.

One of the new opportunities that our regional institute's leadership decided to implement given the new, more localized, structure was to have all corps members complete home visits about halfway through the institute experience. For those who are unfamiliar, typically incoming corps members are assigned to teach one class throughout the summer. The structure varies depending on whether you're teaching elementary or secondary, but corps members are usually in front of students for no less than an hour at a time for at least three to four days out of the week. This particular summer I was assigned to coach and prepare all of the TFA corps members teaching fifth grade at my placement school. They were broken into groups of fours and then split into pairs within those groups. Each pair planned and delivered lessons together, switching off who would take lead. For the first half of the summer, one pair did the English/language arts instruction while the other pair did math/science, and then they swapped for the second half of the summer. I share all of this with you just so you have a little bit of context in terms of how much time corps members spent with their students prior to home visits.

Admittedly, I don't remember how detailed of a briefing the corps members got prior to the home visit, but knowing how Teach For America operates I know there was definitely some sort of discussion prior to sending them off. The corps members were instructed to go to at least one home visit and spend time talking with the families and getting to know them before heading to a nearby school for a pasta dinner and debrief on the home visits covering how it felt to do them, what they learned, and how they can use what they learned to inform their teaching.

While it seemed like many of the corps members enjoyed the home visit activity, and many shared that the students they chose to visit were excited to see them in their home, there were some points where the activity definitely missed the mark. First, to this day, it remains unclear as to whether the families were notified that these home visits were happening. Some of my assigned corps members reported feeling as though their visit was unexpected even as they were welcomed into their students' homes. Now I don't know about you but I don't know many folks who would take kindly to unexpected visitors showing up at their home in the middle of a busy afternoon. In all honesty, I don't even show up to my parents' house without a courtesy "on my way" text. Second, because of the brief nature of the visit in the middle of a summer where they were already spending *hours* quickly ingesting new information on teaching methods, unpacking biases and assumptions, teaching lessons, practicing behavior management techniques, and conducting their own observations of their fellow corps members, it was not clear that they all engaged meaningfully with the families, and some reported that they introduced themselves as the child's teacher, chatted briefly, and left.

In theory, I can see the purpose of conducting home visits and their potential to bridge the home-school culture and foster better communication between teachers and parents/families/caregivers. They're often utilized as a key relationship-building strategy viewed as a way to meet families and students where they are and construct stronger connections between home and school. Proponents of home visits argue that they can serve as a means of building trust between educators and families, foster authentic relationships rooted in trust and care, address potential underlying biases and assumptions, and begin to close the cultural gaps that scholars like

Delpit pinpoint as deeply impacting diverse students' educational experiences and outcomes.

However, given all of these potential benefits and data, many educators and parents are still hesitant. Critics of the practice often find that home visits can feel intrusive with the expectation to meet families in their homes that might open them up to additional ridicule and judgment and can actually cause more damage to the family/teacher relationship. A noted common pitfall in the implementation of home visits is a similar one to calls/notes home. They only occur to address an issue like frequent absences, poor academic performance or behavioral issues. In this sense, the home visit can again feel less like an attempt to build partnership since there has been no previous attempt to enlist familial engagement. Educators in schools and counties that mandate home visits also find that they add an additional responsibility to their already overflowing plates, adding to the burnout they already feel, which can further inhibit their engagement in the process.

Personally, I find that even when these issues are addressed, there is still an imbalance in the intended purpose and practice of home visits. Much of the research on home visits discusses them as an opportunity for families to learn from educators and to bring learning into the home. This automatically views families through a lens of deficit, framing the daily interactions and activities in the home as lacking in educational value.

Attempting to address some of these pitfalls and shortcomings, organizations like the Parent Teacher Home Visit Project (PTHVP) have developed a model for what they call relational home visits. PTHVP was founded in 1998 by a group of parents, community members, and educators who wanted to, as written in their origin story posted to the PTHVP web site, "counter deeply held mistrust and disrupt the cycle of blame between home and school." Initially piloted in eight schools across Sacramento, California, the PTHVP relational home visit model relies on five non-negotiables:

1. **All visits are voluntary and pre-arranged:** The PTHVP found that voluntary activities and programs designed to foster family involvement encourage more active engagement because both parties have

agency in *choosing* when, where, and how they do so. Home visits can be done at the families' actual homes or another location that feels like home to them.

2. **Training and compensation must be provided to participating educators:** To ensure that teachers are prepared to build authentic relationships, they must attend trainings prior to initiating the home visit and are compensated for each visit outside of the school day to "demonstrate value and respect for the commitment."
3. **Visits focus on families' hopes and dreams:** During the first visit, participating educators ask families to share their hopes and dreams for their child/children to set the foundation for a partnership rooted in trust and focused on student success,
4. **Educators visit a cross-section of students:** As previously mentioned, many home visits occur as intervention to address attendance, behavioral, or academic issues with a targeted group of students. In the relational home visit model, found that home visits should be universally offered to all families who express interest.
5. **Educators conduct visits in pairs and engage in ongoing visits and reflections:** Participating educators are expected to engage in ongoing professional learning opportunities through shared reflection and discussion about what they learned about the student and how to incorporate what they've learned into classroom instruction as well as unpacking any previously held biases and assumptions and how those changed as a result. Schools applying the PTHVP model are encouraged to devote portions of staff meetings or professional learning community meetings to collectively debrief and reflect on home visit experiences.

While the PTHVP model does go to some of the greatest lengths to address core issues many opponents, myself included, have with the push for home visits as a relationship-building strategy, one of the fundamental issues that I see with this model is the visits are still very educator/school driven. For example, although the teachers receive training in which they are taught the model and provided with guidance on how to implement it, there is no mention of family or community members specific to the population being served by a particular school being present during these trainings, leaving it unclear how they are preparing educators to meet the *specific* needs and concerns of the communities they serve. Similarly, although there is a great deal that can be gained from collective debriefs and reflections on the experience, if families, or again community members deeply familiar with the specific cultural and historical context, are not present for the collective debriefs, how is it possible to ensure that any lingering misconceptions, biases, and assumptions are adequately addressed?

While the relational model here attempts to provide parents with much more agency in the process, according to a 2017 study and report on PTHV's model, McNight et al. found many of the participating families were unclear about the purpose of the visits and felt teachers received much more guidance and support throughout the process. That being said, additional key findings in the study provided evidence that the relational home visit model is associated with increased incorporation of students' interests and cultures into classroom instruction, and the implementation of empathic disciplinary approaches rather than punitive. Teacher home visits can help to shift dynamics in the family-teacher relationship and encourage more authentic communication between both parties. However, the process must truly be collaborative from start to finish.

Advice from Those with Feet in Both Lanes

When I was thinking about who my featured teachers would be, I immediately knew I wanted to talk with educators who were able to personally speak directly to the tensions of being both a parent and an educator. I was never a parent during my time in the classroom, nor am I at the time of writing this book. However, I've always felt like those educators who *are* parents had a unique level of expertise that we just aren't tapping into enough as we attempt to navigate the family/parent dynamic.

FEATURED TEACHERS: Educators Who Are Also Parents

Brian

During the time [my son] was in school, I was an educator. But there were a whole lot of things that I did not know. I'll be honest. So when looking over some of the homework he had I'd be like "Ah, no, brotha. I mean, I could get somebody to help you, but I don't know." I felt very helpless in that space, of not really being able to help [my son] in the way that I really wanted to. There was also a level of embarrassment because I'm an educator, but sometimes we think that because you're an educator you know everything, which is not always the truth. So I felt, in a real sense, that I needed to know what I didn't know and I thought, how empowering would it be if I did know and I could really help him in the best way possible.

So now, [in my current position] when I thought about translating that to our parents, I realized there are other parents who like me want to help their kids but they don't have the resources. They don't know how. So I was asked to do a workshop during the pandemic, what the, you know, the hybrid pandemic, that would help our parents to understand the MAP testing. Well, we did the workshop, and then after that workshop, I was like we have to continue to do this. The parents were so eager to know how they could help their sons do better on the MAP tests, or what they could do at home to help them [academically], and it drew me right back to that space with [my own son], when I was sitting in the living room, and I'm like, "Yo, brotha, like, we've got to call somebody because I don't know what to do, I want to help, but I don't know what to do."

So we created this parent engagement program that offers yearly workshops; they happen once a month, sometimes, depending upon the year, twice a month, where we're making sure that our parents know how to best support their kids, outside of the classroom space, why literacy is important, how you can help develop language outside of being in the school, and those workshops have been so helpful; our parents are developing the resources and the opportunities to really support their kids in the way that they want to, but they just didn't know how. That's one portion of this family engagement piece. That is important, and I think that is the missing link. Oftentimes, our parents want to support and our educators want parents to support, but there's no system or program or anything around how that actually happens, and so that's why we created this family engagement space. Not only does it serve as this workshop space, but we're also providing support for parents to help their kids outside of the classroom with a lot of different skills, not just academic.

Bobby

I've had to learn very intricately how my kids work, what makes them tick. My son, I can look at him. and he folds and he crumbles. He's like me. He lives in his head a lot. He's me, but an introvert and so for him, knowing that he disappointed me will make him feel bad. He'll keep apologizing. He'll feel like he has to do more and do more [apologizing]. I'm like, "Baby, when you said you were sorry, I'm good. Before you said I'm sorry, we were good. There's nothing that you can do to make me not love you. Nothing." I tell him all the time. My daughter on the other hand, my baby girl, if I look at her, she leans in and looks back. She's an extrovert, but also like my wife, and so she has a loud personality. When she wakes up, everybody gotta get up. You know, like, that's her. My son is an engineer, problem solver, deep thinker, like he's going to change the world in a way where people are gonna be like, "Oh, who made that? He did it." You know, my daughter, she's out in front, you're gonna know she did it, and so when it comes to my daughter, like, in a world that's going to tell a woman when to speak, and how to speak and to shrink, I want to be the voice that says *Speak louder. Let them know you're there.* Restorative justice helps me do that [with my students] because I'm not parenting them, and I'm not diminishing who they are, but helping steer who they are to

(continued)

(continued)

the right things. So now when I go to school, and I'm talking to kids, this is somebody's baby, right? Like I get that intricately because I have to surrender my kids over to the same system, and I had the same concerns.

Reflect and Discuss

1. Both Brian and Bobby shed light on how their *own* journeys with their children deeply inform their practice and relationship with their students' parents/families. Revisit your responses at the start of this chapter. What have your experiences as a parent/caretaker (and/or revelations about your own parents/caretakers) taught you about how to foster more meaningful relationships with your students' parents/families?
2. In Bobby's comments, he states that he's "not parenting" but "steering who [the kids/students] are to the right things." How do you personally interpret this statement? How does it relate to your distinctions between the roles of parents/families/caretakers versus the roles of educators?

Both Brian and Bobby shed light on how reflecting on their journeys with their own children helped them to better understand the needs of their students *and* how to address the concerns of their students' families. Because they both share, or once shared, similar fears and concerns as their students' families, they're able to employ practices that they wished their own children's educators would have and to do so with care and empathy for the *families*. Oftentimes educators place so much emphasis on getting to know their students and developing deep understanding of who *they* are, but I argue that if we are not extending that same energy to the parents we will never truly be able to know and care for our students. Featured teachers Jeff and Tanesha speak directly to the ways in which their own journeys in parenting functioned as a sort of magnifying glass helping them to see *both* their parenting and teaching practices more clearly.

FEATURED TEACHERS: Mirrors and Magnifying Glasses

Jeff

For both of those groups [teachers who are not parents/caregivers and parents/caregivers who are not teachers], you have to be willing to swallow a little bit of pride, and go to sources who you trust and ask questions. If you're an educator, who doesn't have children, go to speak to other educators who have children and just ask like, "Man, I don't have any kids. You have kids, right? Does it affect the way you teach? How? Why? Explain it to me," The same thing goes for parents who aren't educators, when they are interacting with educators. I'm not saying the parents don't know what's in the best interest of their kids; they do. They're the biggest knowledge set about their kids. But if you've never taught, then if what you're seeing doesn't seem to make sense at all, you shouldn't automatically assume that the educator doesn't know what they're doing and jump off and start screaming at them about it. You should be open to also learn at the same time. I'm not saying don't stand up for your child or fight like hell for your child. Yes, do all that. But, learn too. It's a great opportunity for you to model learning to your son or daughter, like, *"Hey, look, I'm learning more about what's going on in your teacher's class, through my communication with them and by asking them questions and them answering and then he asked more questions and we started to go back and forth, and we both get to a point where we learn more about each other, and we learn more about certain issues, and we learn better how to help you."* That's a great way to model it to your son or daughter, like, *"Hey, this is what you should be doing when you're in his class too. You should be asking questions and having good discussions with him, sharing your thoughts about things. Then, you know, everybody learns, me included."*

Tanesha

Yeah, I would say to [educators] who are not parents, my first thing would be like, you can't and should not try to do it all. And what I mean by that is like, you should not feel like you have to pick up the weight, you should not

(continued)

(continued)

feel like because you don't have a kid, you have to do more. Capitalism will make you feel a lot of different ways, and it's not on you, that's the system. Enjoy your free time and a lot of it too, because it's free, it's yours, you're not getting paid for it. I want [educators] without kids to realize that this is just your job. It is just a job. I think that for families who are not educators, I think, the understanding that for teachers, it is their job and then that comes with real boundaries. Respect those boundaries that teachers put in place knowing that they want a relationship with you. I've never met a teacher who was just like, I don't want a relationship with this family. Right? I *have* heard teachers say, "This is really hard, it is challenging, our relationship is strained, we don't have the best relationship," but I've never heard people say "I don't want a relationship." Just also know your child whom you're advocating for is one of maybe 30, 60, 90, 120 whom their teacher is receiving. So just keep that both/and type of mindset. The teacher should get back to you, *and* your beautiful child is also one of *many* that this teacher is trying to respond to, and perhaps in addition to the ones that they might have *at home* that they're trying to be there for as well. So I think you've got to hold up the mirror, in that moment to see both sides, the mirror and a magnifying glass. The mirror is like *I can see the teacher in myself* and the magnifying glass is *I'm still gonna go hard on you teacher because this is my child.*

Reflect and Discuss

1. Reflecting on the examples and advice that Jeff and Tanesha provide, think of some examples of when applying your role as either parent or teacher through a mirror AND magnifying glass could have created a more positive interaction and a meaningful outcome for the student?
2. Teachers who ARE ALSO parents/caregivers to school-aged children, reflect on the following: What do you think parents/caretakers who are not teachers *and* teachers who are not parents/caretakers tend to misunderstand and/or overlook? How do your dual identities as both parent/caretaker and educator inform how you engage with your students' parents/caretakers *and* your children's teachers?

As I listened to and reflected on all of the wisdom from our featured teachers who shared about their journeys in teaching and parenting, one thing came through clearly: their practices with other people's children is fueled by an understanding that every parent just wants to know that their child is being cared for and loved, especially when they're not around. Sure, navigating partnerships with parents/caretakers is challenging, especially for those of us who haven't taken on that particular identity in our life's journey. However, speaking from experience what I can tell you is at the *root* of all, and maybe to play it safe I'll say most, parents'/caregivers' engagements in their children's educational journeys is a deep love and desire for them to be safe, to be happy, to be whole, and to be seen/valued/respected/loved for who they are.

Conclusion

In this chapter, we explored the important role that parents/caretakers play in coming to know who our students are. As with other aspects of our instruction, many educators enter classrooms with pre-conceived notions of how "good" or "effective" parental/caretaker involvement should look. These pre-conceived notions are often woven together from the experiences, both positive and negative, that we had with our own parents/caretakers throughout our educational journeys *and* the representations of parenting that we see portrayed in movies, television, news, and so on. While home visits are often pushed as an effective strategy to bridge home and school, my hope is that the comprehensive overview and critique of the PTHV model helps to illuminate some of the complexities and nuances that need to be considered *before, during, and after* implementing them in your school or district. Above anything else, when considering the use of home visits, the primary question to ask and continuously reflect on is: *why do we want to do home visits and what evidence do we have that they will be an effective means to that end?*

The continued framing of parents/caretakers as barriers serves no one, particularly students, and further dehumanizes everyone in the process. As discussed in this chapter, the use of students and their parents/caretakers as political pawns fuels a divisive narrative that *does* create a barrier to providing the educational experiences that our nation's students deserve. If we listen to the perspectives of those who are already moving through an identity woven together from their perspectives as *both* parent and educator, we might find the keys to tapping into everyone's humanity and weaving together dynamic and collaborative learning environments.

REVISITING CRITICAL AUTOBIOGRAPHIES: Perspectives on Parents/Caretakers

Return to your Critical Educational Autobiography, reflect on the following questions, and add the new information to the appropriate sections:

1. Reflecting on your own K–12 experiences, what messages did you internalize about what "good," "positive," or "effective" parental/caregiver involvement looks like? (This might be different at various stages of the educational process so reflect on that as well.)
2. How did, or might, these narratives shape your relationship-building practices with your students' parents/caretakers? Whom might these narratives automatically favor? Whom might they unfairly exclude?

References

Delpit, L. (2006). *Other People's Children: Cultural Conflict in the Classroom*. The New Press.

McKnight, K., Venkateswaran, N., Laird, J., Robles, J., & Shalev, T. (2017). *Mindset Shifts and Parent Teacher Home Visits*. RTI International.

Chapter 9

Weaving It All Together

Remember: Your practice can be a space to show and give YOURSELF the love you need and deserve.

Tweet and Instagram Post
@drcourtneyrose (February 2, 2022)

Most of us have heard the saying "hurt people hurt people," which succinctly and powerfully communicates the tendency for folks to spread unexplored, unprocessed, and unhealed pain and trauma from either their past or present to those around them. This manifests in a myriad of ways, but one of the more common examples is a child who experiences physical or emotional abuse/ridicule in the home, then coming to school and engaging in similar acts with children they deem as weaker in some way. When exploring how various aspects of one's experiences with schools and schooling manifest in their instructional and leadership practices, I break down this saying into more specific components: silenced people silence people, and dehumanized people dehumanize people. By design, the normative and standardized practices dominating within the public school system are both fueled by and fueling deficit-based narratives, conditioning many of us to focus primarily (or solely) on what we, and others, *don't* have and *can't* do in the process.

Throughout this book, you were encouraged to weave together the experiences and narratives that informed the development of your identity and practice as an educator. In the process, you may have unraveled some of the dehumanizing narratives, policies, and practices that led to you silencing, hiding, or otherwise downplaying aspects of yourself in order to successfully navigate educational spaces and society at large. While many of us come to terms with some of the ways that we may have internalized negative messages about ourselves, as educators we don't always take, or feel like we have, the time to critically reflect on how these underlying beliefs may be manifesting in our own practice as we take on the identity of one who teaches.

In the preparation of critical multicultural and culturally relevant educators, the necessity for critical self-reflection remains at the core of the work. Developing effective *and* affirming strategies for today's students is contingent upon critical reflection about race and culture of teachers *in relation to* our students. Specifically, it requires that teachers are equipped with the necessary skills to critically reflect on our own racial and cultural identities and to recognize how these identities coexist with the cultural compositions of our students. In other words, when we have a better understanding of who we are we can better understand how to weave that together with who our students are to develop learning environments that are spun from our unique assets rather than our perceived deficits.

Scholar and teacher educator, Howard Milner (2003) emphasizes the importance of this explicit reflection on race and culture within teacher education programs due to the prevalence of an oppressive colorblind ideology within the increasingly diverse education system that has strong implications for the instructional practices of teachers of all racial and cultural backgrounds. According to Milner (2003), critical reflection can help White teachers who have adopted colorblind ideologies unearth the silencing and alienating impact such beliefs have on learning among students of color. Further, teachers of color need to reflect on issues of race and contexts to examine the oppressive misconceptions and White supremacist ideologies they often operate through as a result of their own teaching and learning experiences that can often feel even *more* oppressive and alienating to students who come from similar racial and cultural backgrounds.

Looking to their own experiences as teachers and teacher educators, critical multicultural and culturally relevant scholars acknowledge the personal and institutional barriers that can often cause difficulty in this process.

Thus, these scholars provide a number of techniques through which to alleviate the personal strain that is often associated with the process, while pushing for deep critical analysis of the sociopolitical forces at play. Like me, Ladson-Billings (2000) suggests the use of autobiography as an approach to fostering this type of deep reflection. This approach allows teachers to critically examine their experiences of difference in and outside of the classroom and to speak as subjects in their own voice. Thus the use of autobiography in teacher education functions as a tool through which to assist teachers in development of a critical consciousness while also serving as a model for the type of student engagement called for within theories of culturally relevant pedagogy.

Creating Communities of Learning

Prevalent within the discussion of preparing educators to teach in culturally and linguistically diverse settings is the creation of systems of support for teachers in these settings to facilitate high-quality educational experiences. Increasing the effectiveness and inclusiveness of these reflective communities, I also argue that they should include the voices and perspectives of parents/caregivers *and* students. Previous research fueled the development of spaces where teachers working in, and preparing to work in, culturally diverse environments have the opportunity to come together and grapple with the various techniques for overcoming the context-specific barriers they may face in their work environments. Further, they suggest that providing such space for these *communities of learning* opens up opportunities for theory and practice to intersect and dynamic, transformative pedagogical practices to emerge. However, as discussed in Chapters 7 and 8, too often these communities are developed without authentic, honest, and/or consistent contribution from parents/caretakers and students reinforcing messages that devalue their presence in the learning community and allow pre-existing divides to persist and grow.

Through her exploration of attempting to create this environment within a university setting, bell hooks (1993) exposes the fear-based resistance or hesitancy to adjusting teaching practices in the multicultural classroom. The transformative, democratic pedagogical practices that hooks calls for often brings up fear of loss of control within the classroom as it opens doors to critique and less control as to what topics gain entry into the learning environment, a fear that many might argue came to fruition in the wake of the large-scale shift to virtual learning between 2020 and 2021 that enabled more parents/caregivers to gain unfiltered access to their children's learning experiences. However, as explored in Chapter 7, opening up the learning space in a way that makes room for values and affirms and constructively critiques *all* members of the learning community's voices can provide a more liberating and transformative experience for teacher, student, and parent/caretaker as all become responsible for the learning that takes place (hooks, 1993). As a note to teacher educators, providing teachers with a similar collaborative environment, in both the pre- and in-service experiences, opens up opportunities for collaboration through the sharing and creation of strategies and approaches and collective reflection on these practices in a supportive environment. This can also alleviate feelings of isolation that are associated with the individualistic, "behind closed doors" approach to teaching that often serves as a barrier for new teachers and those looking to enact more culturally relevant practices and has played a major role in the recent mass exodus from the classroom.

In their discussion of properly preparing teachers for work in culturally diverse urban environments, Oakes et al. (2002) suggest that the use of the aforementioned communities of learning can help teachers look beyond traditional university-based and district-mandated teacher education/professional development experiences to gain necessary knowledge and skills. In doing so, teachers learn to view students, parents, colleagues, and various community members as experts with whom they should frequently consult in the process of shaping their pedagogical practices. Additionally, as they engage in a continuous process of collective critical self-reflection and dialogue, they may be able to more easily identify their own power cords (see Chapter 2) that will enable them to weave together practices from a place of power rather than fear.

Teaching as Love, Healing, and Resistance

Deeply engaging with your own identity development processes opens pathways to explore the ways who you are, who you want to become, and who you maybe haven't come to terms with yet are all woven into your practice. If done with fidelity and honesty, it can reveal ways to enact and embody your role and identity as one who teaches to develop spaces rooted in love, healing, and resistance that creates powerful waves in your life extending beyond the walls of your classroom. Featured teacher Yari speaks to this aspect of her journey as she wove together the pieces of her teacher identity that manifested in many different aspects of her life and world.

FEATURED TEACHERS: Love, Healing and Resistance

Yari

I made the distinction between formal teachers and also informal teachers, because I feel like there are so many people, there are so many beings that are teachers in this world, and in my life, that are horrible teachers in a classroom and have taught me in many different ways. And so I feel like, I make the distinction between formal teaching and the career of teaching and also being a teacher because, even when I am not in my space, or my formal space of teaching, or in my career space of teaching, I am always teaching whether I am teaching as a mother, whether I am teaching as a partner, whether I am teaching as a sister, whether I am teaching as a granddaughter, whether I am teaching as a niece, you know, I feel like we are and I feel like everyone is a teacher, to be honest with you, I feel like we are always teaching. It depends what lessons we get from moments of teaching that can either be harmful, can either be incredibly transformative. And so right now in my life, I take that responsibility, very deeply in whatever space that I am in as a teacher, to be very responsible with that sort of mindset. It's the reason why I speak of

(continued)

(continued)

love so boldly and so courageously because that anchors me, you know, when navigating different emotions that come even when we are teaching or in teachable moments. So, you know, I am a teacher; I think we are teachers, but I am also a formal career educator that has been educated also in a pipeline, where we've all been mis-educated. And so I'm also a mis-educated teacher, trying to relearn how to be a critically conscious you know, loving teacher now, in my way of being.

Yari's use of the term *mis-educated* immediately took me to a place that I am honestly surprised I didn't come to until now. My ALL TIME favorite album is Lauryn Hill's 1998 album, *The Miseducation of Lauryn Hill*, which to date remains her only studio album. I was only 13 when this album was released, and if I'm being honest I don't remember the first time I heard it. In fact, I don't think I paid much attention to it until years later. *Miseducation* was the soundtrack of the majority of my high school years, and although the album's themes focus mostly on things I had little-to-know experience with (i.e., romantic love and motherhood), I was deeply connected with the emotion and storytelling. Later, as I became better acquainted with the content of what Lauryn's lyrics covered, I realized that the entire album was a journey in identity development, of unlearning and relearning who one is, which makes sense if you consider that the album title was inspired by Carter G. Woodson's *The Miseducation of the Negro* (1933), in which Woodson argues that Black people of his time were culturally indoctrinated within American schools into believing that they were inferior, resulting in them becoming dependent and seeking lower level positions within society. Woodson urges readers to "do for themselves" as a means of disrupting this miseducation.

Woven throughout the album are interludes of a "teacher," played by poet Ras Bakara, speaking with who we are meant to presume are his students in a classroom. The conversation, which actually took place in Hill's living room, focuses on love, completely driven by the students' definitions, conceptualizations, and experiences of it. Speaking to how these classroom scenes build the connection between her work and Woodson's, editor and freelance writer Paul Schrodt had this to say in a 2008 review of the album for *Slant*: "[Hill] adopts Woodson's thesis and makes it part of her own artistic process. Like the songs themselves, the intro/outro classroom scenes suggest a larger community working to redefine itself." Hill echoed this sentiment herself in a special message shared in a since-deleted YouTube video, stating: ". . .it has a lot to do with finding out about your own aspirations and your own dreams, and not those dreams and those aspirations that some might have for you. It's a song about movement and growth and inspiration."

Similarly, I find that many of us have been miseducated on the true purpose and role of the "formal teacher" who has strong roots in our own miseducation of who we are (to reiterate Yari's powerful language). Engaging in processes of deep critical self-reflection can help you unravel this miseducation that is often interlaced with threads of fear, doubt, and shame that stem from an overemphasis in individualistic competition rather than collective growth and development. As the famous proverb states: if you want to go fast, go alone, but if you want to go far, go together. Together, as a collective community of teachers, learners, parents/caregivers, all weaving in and out of those roles and leaning into our power and strength, we can redefine and reweave a new vision for our work as one rooted in love, healing, and resistance.

Advice for the Next Generation of Teachers or Those Debating Whether or Not to Stay

As mentioned throughout this text, I wrote this book in the midst of one of the largest teacher shortages in U.S. history. As a teacher educator myself, who finds herself engaging with over 100 pre- and in-service teachers every week, I often see them becoming weighed down or begin to waver in their commitments and decisions to become educators. I remember this feeling all too well from my own journey in the K–12 classroom. I also acknowledge that as you all have engaged in a similar (well, nearly identical actually) process of self-reflection that I take my students through in my courses, you may be starting to feel the same impacts of coming face-to-face with the realities woven into the work that cause some of these questions and concerns to arise. Therefore, just as I do with my students, I am going to close this book with a final bit of motivation and encouragement from the field. Specifically, during my conversations with each of the featured teachers whose stories were woven throughout this text, I ended the interview by asking them to share their words of encouragement and advice for the next generation of teachers or to those who may be wavering in their decision to become one who teaches. Here is what Joscelyn, Jeff, Dee, and Eva had to say.

FEATURED TEACHERS: Advice for the Next Generation

Joscelyn

I have all of these sayings that I have grown to love over the years. There is one that I constantly keep coming back to because it really embodies the opportunity. Even with teachers feeling very vulnerable in their decision to be an educator, at this moment, there is still this incredible opportunity if they are willing to see it. In order to see it, they have to see their kids, but then see how expansive their lives will become. That is when teaching still is so powerful and inspiring and joyful because it is not just about you going into the classroom.

One thing that I always say is that "we don't teach students for our classrooms, we teach them to leave it." It is like the essence of everything that I have learned, and what I want teachers to just hold onto. It is not about this standard, this lesson. The students are not going to remember any of that really. It is going to be all one big blur, but they will not forget how you made them feel. They will not forget the character shifts because that stuff stands out. It stands out the first time you were empowered to use your voice and you spoke up in class. Like that is like a moment that changed you as a person. They will remember those things. I have students coming back and they do not remember the exact lesson.

They just remembered the joy. Yeah. And that is a requirement now for their environments. That is a requirement for their relationships.

They remember the trust that we had, who they are, and that spreads out into who they become in their communities. That is what it is all about. That is really what it is all about. And so if you can just see past the immediate challenges, the lack of resources, the lack of funds, the lack of compensation, if you can see past it, or you cannot even see past it, I might not even see past it, you know that it is there. But what is also true and what is also there is that great opportunity to impact communities and kids' character and lives beyond that. It is so awesome to tap into if you expand your lessons to include that sort of mindset. It is so fun. . .and the evolution of little leaders that who are just able to advocate for themselves like, so crazy.

Jeff

I mean, it's a profession that has lots of issues now. It probably always has, but the onslaught of so many new things that are popping up in society now makes it even harder to understand. But I guess what I would say as a way to try to incentivize them or encourage them to stay in it is that I really can't think of a more rewarding career. And I can't think of another career that can have a direct and immediate and long-lasting effect on the life and mind and psyche of a young person. You know, whether these pre-service teachers are thinking about teaching pre-K or 12th graders. It doesn't matter. All those students are young people.

And, I mean, if you are human, I mean, we all need to make money. We all need to make money to support ourselves and buy food and shelter. But really, what's going to be the most beneficial thing in your life is if you have a way to, positively serve others. I made a lot of money, I made a lot of money, working in finance for all those years, 20 years, and I was good at it and all that stuff, but it was killing me. I was dying, I was aging, I was just having all the happiness drained out to make it very

(continued)

(continued)

rote, that's the other thing. It was a very rote existence, like, they do the same things every month, on the same days, it just keeps going over and over and over.

Teaching's not rote ever. You never know what's going to happen. And on any day, in any class period, you're gonna have a great plan. And, you know, something could happen that in the first two minutes of the class blows the plan up, and you have to, you know, fix it on the fly. So I think if you are the kind of person who enjoys the challenge of figuring out problems, in the immediacy and like, on your feet, and having to come up with it, getting challenged to come up with an answer and fix something right away, then, you know, it's a great profession.

Diedra

I think this is the number one advice I have. I realize that they have the power to really be the change, right. Everything that is happening in education. I believe that this new generation of teachers is going to be the one that is going to because they are hearing it. They are seeing, and now it is a thing. So they are really the ones who can be the advocates that we need. And so there is a certain level of, yes, you are the change, right? Your students need you.

I would also say, find your community, and not go into it expecting your school to be your be all and end all because it is not going to be. It is not going to be the only place for Professional Development (PD), it is not going to be the only place for friendship and community and all that. And so sometimes, it might require you to get out of your comfort zone, and find your people who can help you to really make peace with the decision that you are making.

Then I will also say that there is a certain level of, when you will meet your students, I think that is what really shifts things. Where it is like, you see that they are not just not random students. These are the students who are in your classroom. They have names. They have lives. They have smiles. They have energy. They are funny. I think that there is something to be said about really knowing that you are going to truly make a positive impact in their lives. As cheesy as that sounds, I think that is a powerful thing.

I guess, the fear that I have sometimes is that if we are losing so many teachers who is going to be teaching our children? Who is going to be teaching them? So, I mean, that would be the advice I would give. I know it is a tough time. It is definitely a tough time. And the last thing I would say too, is to really make it a priority to strengthen your own communication skills. Find your voice. Learn how to be assertive. Learn how to be able to identify your boundaries and communicate those things. Do not sleep on the communication skills because you are going to be in situations where you are really going to need it. And so, I would say to make that a priority as well.

Eva

I would say find a mentor. Find someone who can continue to remind you of your why and why you do this work and find and create opportunities for you to experience joy every single day. Peloton has saved my life. I will advocate for a Peloton for the rest of my life. I am obsessed. I am one of those people. I love it so, so, so, much. But that brings me joy almost every single day, whether it is meditation or a yoga class, it is something that brings me joy just for myself, and then reminding myself to create joy in the classroom every single day. I have that as a sticky note on my computer. Smile, whatever it is, even if you are having a bad day, figure out how you use the classroom to make it a better day.

My big thing is to close your door and forget all the BS, because we are not—you are not going to go into a school that is lit and amazing and great and fantastic all of the time. There are going to be issues with whatever school you go into, and you are going to want to create change in those schools. But do not ever become complacent. Do not be complacent. This is just how it is. Fight to make things change, but also recognize

(continued)

(continued)

that you do not do it to the detriment of yourself, and so when you are in the classroom, do not bring the BS of the school into the classroom with you. Close the door.

They could be a mess. Your classroom does not have to be a mess, and that was something that someone said to me as I moved into this school. They can be disorganized. You do not have to be disorganized. They can be a mess. You do not have to be a mess. That was a real game-changer for me, of recognizing that, yeah, all of these things are true. The school is a hot mess. They are not doing this right. They are not doing that right. All of that is true. But you do have access and autonomy over your thoughts and your choices.

I do not know that there is another job that will be as rewarding as this one. A week into summer break, and I miss my students. There are not a lot of jobs where you are going to go on vacation and say that you miss the job that you do. But, it is about how you do the job during the year. That I know. There are a lot of teachers who say, "I am glad we're not in the classroom with kids all summer." Although I am glad, and I am getting my rest, I am happy about it. I would hate to think that I am not going to be in front of students engaging with students ever again.

That would be horrible.

References

hooks, b. (1993). Transformative pedagogy and multiculturalism. In T. Perry & J. Fraser (Eds.), *Freedom's plow: Teaching in the multicultural classroom* (pp. 91–97). Routledge.

Ladson-Billings, G. (2000). Fighting for our lives: Preparing teachers to teach African American students. *Journal of Teacher Education*, *51*(3), 206–214. doi:10.1177/0022487100051003008

Milner, R. H. (2003). Teacher reflection and race in cultural contexts: History, meanings, and methods in teaching. *Theory Into Practice*, *42*, 173–180. doi:10.2307/1477417

Oakes, J., Franke, M. L., Quartz, K. H., & Rogers, J. (2002). Research for high-quality urban teaching: Defining it, developing it, assessing it. *Journal of Teacher Education*, *53*(3), 228–235.

Ruffhouse. (1998). *The miseducation of lauryn hill.*

Schrodt, P. (2008, August 20). Review of *The miseducation of lauryn hill. Slant Magazine.* Retrieved from https://www.slantmagazine.com/music/lauryn-hill-the-miseducation-of-lauryn-hill/.

Woodson, C. G. (1933). *The miseducation of the negro.* The Associated Publishers.

Appendix 1

Critical Educational Autobiography Assignment

For Educators/Facilitators: This is the actual written instructions for the Critical Educational Autobiography assignment that I use in all of my courses. This could also be used for professional development sessions or by school administrators seeking to do some relationship and community-building activities. As written, the assignment is designed for use with college-aged students/adults, however it can easily be tweaked for use with younger students.

An important focus of this course is to understand the intersection of culture, society, schools, classrooms, and individuals. This assignment provides an opportunity for you to reflect on yourself as a culture bearer and on the influence of education in your life. We each have a narrative that defines us to date. That narrative has many aspects and is your story. In your writing, address the following as your story to date. Use the following questions to build your narrative.

The aim of the Critical Educational Autobiography is to explore key experiences, inside and outside of school, that have shaped who you are as a person, and your journey into teaching. As you write, discuss the following:

1. Identity: How do you identify with regards to race, class, gender, sexual orientation, language, and/or ability? What privileges do you have and/or barriers do you face because of these identities (both inside and outside of school)?

- What are some key life (out-of-school) events that shaped your views about your social, cultural, and academic identities?

2. Key Educational Experiences: What are some key educational experiences that shaped your views about teaching and learning, the role of the educator, and the purpose of education?
   - Identify and discuss some positive AND negative learning/teaching experiences and how they have shaped you as a learner and informed the type of educator you hope to become.
3. Social/Political Context: Discuss some of the major social & political movements/events that occurred during your schooling years. These could be local, state and/or national. How, if at all did they shape or impact conversations about/within education? How, if at all, did they impact your experiences within schools and/or your vision for yourself as an educator or in your future roles?
4. Journey into Teaching/Your Chosen Career: Who/what shaped your beliefs about the goals of education, the role of teachers, and your vision for yourself as an educator?
   - What key people impacted your experiences as a learner and peaked your interest in becoming a teacher or entering your chosen career?
   - What do you hope to accomplish as an educator/in your future role?

It is important to dig deeply and critically reflect in order to identify some of the internalized messages and beliefs that may be impacting your views on teaching and learning. However, only share what you feel comfortable sharing.

You may present your autobiography in any of the following formats, however you must explain at some point why you chose to present your narrative in this way:

- Written Paper (could be a straightforward writing of your story or a more creative short story format as if someone else was telling your story).
- PowerPoint, Prezi, Google Slides, FlipGrid, or some other similar format of a presentation.
- Video (either sitting or talking straight into the camera or a more documentary-style or creative film) or Audio (think podcast).
- Poem, Song, Cartoon, Drawing, or some other artistic representation (may require a short written piece to explain).

Appendix 2

"What's in a Name?" Discussion

For Instructors/Facilitators: This is an activity that I use at the beginning of every course that I teach. It helps me to begin to get to know who is in the room, serves as a powerful relationship/community-building tool between the students and myself (I share my story as well), and opens up dialogue that covers important concepts related to identity and our experiences within schools and society that are important to the course itself. This could be used to open professional development sessions as well, or by administrators who want to build community among their teachers and staff. Additionally, with some tweaks, it could also be used with students, particularly those in middle and high school.

Student Prep Prior to Lesson/Activity

Throughout [class/course/workshop], we will spend a lot of time exploring and reflecting on our identities and the people and experiences (both inside and outside) of schools that have shaped them. Understanding who we are and how we see and are seen in the world can help us to better understand and interpret some of the policies and practices we've seen/experienced in schools and the ways certain events may have felt or impacted our lives.

A core component of who we are is our names, so that is where we are going to start. BEFORE [class/we meet] next week, take some time to research your NAME STORY. You won't have to turn anything in, but we will break into groups and share our name stories with each other (yes, I am going to share my name story with all of you) so you may want to write things down to have to refer to during our class/session discussion.

Here are some questions for you to think about as you do your research.

> NOTE: You may not have access to or feel comfortable sharing responses to all of these questions. That's perfectly fine, and you should only share what you feel safe and comfortable sharing.

- What does your name mean? What are the origins of your name (geographically and culturally)?
- Who gave you your name and why did they choose that name for you?
- Have you always had the same name? When or why did it change? How did you feel before and after it changed?
- Do you go by your given name or do you use a nickname or some other family name that you either selected or was given to you? Explain.
- Do you feel like your name suits you? Explain.

Instructions during the Lesson/Activity

In your breakout groups, share your "Name Story." You can use the following prompts to guide your discussion.

> NOTE: I encourage educators/facilitators to share THEIR name story to the whole group first. This not only serves as a model, but also has a tendency to open up the participants because the educator/facilitator leads with vulnerability and trust).

- I was given my name because. . .
- I like/dislike my name because. . .
- My name is/isn't a good fit for my personality because. . .
- What might your name tell others about your identity? What stories about you or your family might your name reflect? What about your identity is simplified, hidden, or confused by your name?

- Describe a time when someone made an assumption about you because of your name.

After everyone shares, discuss the following:

- How are names related to our personal histories? How might they be related to our national history?
- Are names the same as who we are? How much changes when your name changes?

Show any or all of the following videos:

- "Unforgettable" by Pages Matam, Elizabeth Acevedo & G. Yamazawa
- Brainstuff: "Does Your Name Determine Your Future?"
- Vox: "Why Mispronouncing a Name Can Undermine a Student's Identity—and How to Help"

Post-Lesson/Activity Debrief/ Discussion Questions

> NOTE: These questions are displayed or handed out to students/participants at the end of the activity. Depending on time, groups can discuss them before holding a whole group discussion or you can just head straight into a whole group debrief. There is also an option to turn this into a more formal assignment that students/participants submit as an exit ticket of sorts, but there should still be some collective debriefing of the activity.

- What do you think the purpose of this activity was?
- What key takeaways are you leaving with?
- Would you recommend this activity to be used with/by teachers and students in schools? Why or why not?

Appendix 3

Policy Analysis/Reflection Assignment

> **For Educators/Facilitators:** Throughout the book, I discuss many state and national bills/policies that have impacted the experiences of teachers and students within schools. During the 2021–2022 school year, I developed the following Education Policy Analysis/Reflection activity to guide my pre-service teachers in the process of analyzing and reflecting on some of the state policies that were causing them concerns about how they would be able to enact their practice. Besides other teacher educators, this could be a helpful activity for educators to use on an individual, small group, or school-wide basis to do some of the similar analysis and reflection, and gain a deeper understanding of policies in *their* district or state. It could also be used by high school (or maybe even middle school) educators who want to encourage their students to engage in similar policy analysis.

Education Policy Analysis/Reflection

Whether you plan on teaching in the classroom or not, education policies/bills can, and often do, have major impacts, sparking intense dialogue and making waves in other sectors of society. It's important to develop skills to analyze these policies/bills and begin to reflect on how they may shape dialogue and practices within education and beyond. For this assignment, you will select a recently passed bill (I've listed two of the recent ones making waves in Florida, but feel free to focus on any state of your choice—the bill just has to have been passed within the last three to five years) and analyze/reflect on it in relation to some of the topics and issues we've discussed in this course.

Use the following guidelines as a "checklist" for your reflection.

Part 1: Summarize

- What are the key points of the bill? These must come DIRECTLY from the bill itself, not secondary reports, although you can certainly read those to help you better understand what the bill says.
- Has the bill evolved or changed over time? If so, what sparked these changes?
- What do PROPONENTS of the bill say? Again, these should be pulled directly from news reports or interviews, NOT your personal opinion of their thoughts and feelings or what you THINK proponents are thinking. For this first section, you just want to explore what has been said and written without any of your own personal analysis. That will come in the analyze and reflect section.
- What do OPPONENTS of the bill say?

Part 2: Analyze and Reflect

- What assumptions or dominant narratives is the bill grounded in? Look for positive AND negative assumptions/narratives.
- Which key stakeholders in education does this bill impact (educators, students, parents, school board officials, etc.)? Keep in mind that it could, and most likely does, impact more than one of these groups if not all of them. Be specific about HOW it does or might impact them both positively AND negatively.
- Whose voices, perspectives, and experiences does the bill prioritize and amplify? Whose voices, perspectives, and experiences does the bill potentially diminish, silence, or ignore?

- Personal connections/reflections (questions to consider—don't feel the need to touch on ALL of them):
  - What gives you hope about the bill (if anything), and why?
  - What concerns you the most about the bill, and why? How do you personally connect with this bill?
  - How do you think it will or should impact your future practice and/or the ways educators, students, parents, and so on engage in schools/the educational process?
  - What additional questions or points for further discussion do you want to pose or plan to continue reflecting on and researching?

Assignment/Activity Checklist

- Was I thorough? Did I write at least three to five pages, and did I submit on time? (4 points)
- Did I connect my analysis and reflection to some of the major key ideas and issues in the course readings/videos? Did I incorporate the ideas, quotes, and/or examples from at least three to five readings/videos? (4 points)
- Did I make connections to personal experiences and/or other major social and political events? (4 points)
- Did I discuss how this will this impact my own teaching practice or pursuits in education? Give examples, if possible. (4 points)
- Did I pose a clear/non-rhetorical question or points for further discussion—at any point during my reflection? (4 points)

Appendix 4

Classroom Management Philosophy and Action Plan

This is the detailed write-up of the instructions for the culturally relevant classroom management plan that was discussed in Chapter 7. It was originally developed for use in a secondary classroom management course and assigned in two parts: the classroom management philosophy and action plan. Either of these components can be broken up into subcomponents or smaller assignments, depending on your course/professional development workshop timeline. Just use the headings to guide you (i.e., Part 1 contains four components, Parts 1.1–1.4, and each of these can be submitted as separate mini assignments).

Culturally Relevant Classroom Management Plan

Part 1

The key aim of this course/workshop series is to develop an initial Classroom/Behavior Management Plan. This assignment addresses the Statement of Purpose component of the plan. However, it expands on traditional conceptualizations of the statement of purpose, requiring teacher candidates to develop a more comprehensive picture of their classroom management philosophy. The classroom management philosophy section should address the teacher candidate's views on the following items.

Part 1.1: Beliefs about Students

- Do you believe that students need to be "controlled and disciplined" or that they can (and need to) be taught self-control?
- Do you think that students are naturally disruptive, and therefore, need to be molded or conditioned to behave appropriately?
- Do you view students as equals or as charges?
- To what degree do you believe students should be involved in the development, presentation, and implementation of classroom rules, procedures, and daily classroom management practices?

Part 1.2: Beliefs about Teacher's Role

- Do you see yourself as a boss or more as a guide? Are you more of a facilitator or a delegator?
- What is your view on creating rules? Should the teacher make them all or should it they be negotiated with the students?
- Are you more of an assertive educator or do you think teachers should be more laid back?
- Is the teacher the leader, or do you think the students should have a say in what or how they learn?
- What is your belief on discipline? Should students have a say?
- Do you believe that teachers should spend time at the beginning of the year to teach rules and procedures?

Part 1.3: Beliefs/Views of Managing a Classroom

- Do you believe in establishing an authoritarian, permissive, or democratic atmosphere? What does that look, sound, feel like?
- What is the purpose of classroom management?
- What does a well-managed classroom environment look like?
- What is your view on disruptive behavior?
- What is your belief on rewarding students for good behavior?

- Are you okay with using the school system's behavior management plan, or do you want to adopt your own because you have a different perspective?

Part 1.4: Reflections on Community and Communication

- How do you believe your classroom management philosophy will work to provide your students with a safe and supportive environment?
- How do you plan on getting to know your students? Is this a necessary component? Why or why not?
- How do you plan on communicating your philosophy and behavioral expectations with families? Is this a necessary component? Why or why not?

> NOTE: The preceding questions (adapted from: https://www.theedadvocate.org/writing-a-philosophy-of-classroom-management-and-classroom-management-plan/) should serve as guides to help in the development of the classroom management philosophy. Teacher candidates are not required to answer each individual question, however they MUST touch on each of the three *components* (students' role, teacher's role, views on managing a classroom).

Part 2

This section addresses the action plan, which explores how teacher candidates plan to maintain their learning community and manage behavior on a daily basis. The action plan should include the following items.

Part 2.1: Classroom Climate

Describe the culture and climate you hope to foster in your future classroom through the implementation of the system of proactive management you propose in the following sections. Provide specific examples of how the proposed plans communicate and foster respect for students' cultural, linguistic, and family backgrounds at the individual and whole class levels. Additionally, discuss the strategies you plan to employ to maintain a positive classroom climate for *all* students that includes openness, inquiry, fairness, and support. Provide artifacts that show respect and create a positive, safe, productive, and engaging environment for all, including how you plan to communicate with parents/families.

Part 2.2: System of Proactive Management

Describe and provide examples of two to three incentives you plan to implement to promote and maintain positive and productive behavior and academic engagement. Then, discuss and provide examples of the methods and strategies you will use to prevent and respond to disruptive or unproductive behavior and academic disengagement. Create some sort of visual that shows how you plan on displaying and communicating this system to students and the rationale for how these specific strategies will help to maintain the learning community, goals, and aims you discussed in your statement of purpose. You should address both your incentives and consequences at the following levels:

- Individual.
- Whole Class.
- Small Group.

Be sure to provide citations and references from course materials and additional sources to provide evidence and support for your rationale and use of your proposed system of proactive management.

Part 2.3: High Expectations/Teacher Behaviors

Briefly describe how you plan to communicate and hold your students to high academic and behavioral expectations. As you will most likely touch on this throughout the discussion of your rules, procedures, and proactive management system, this section may be woven throughout the others and does not need to be its own standalone section. However, within this portion of your management plan you should focus heavily on the specific *teacher behaviors* that you will employ and monitor to ensure that you are explicitly and implicitly communicating high expectations. These might include but are not limited to:

- Reflexive Teaching.
- Collaborative Efforts.
- Communicative Practices.

Be sure to provide citations and references from course materials and additional sources to provide evidence and support for your rationale and use of your proposed strategies of maintaining and communicating high expectations and how they promote self-directed and collaborative learners.

Part 2.4: Differentiation/Accommodations

Discuss and provide *specific* examples of how you plan to accommodate and/or differentiate either the presentation, teaching, or implementation of your daily management action plan to meet the needs of diverse students in order to promote and maintain a positive, safe, productive, and engaging learning environment that holds *all* students to high expectations.

Index

Page numbers followed by *f* refer to figures.